SEAN

LEARY'S

GREATEST

HITS

VOLUME TEN:

OF TIGER KINGS AND COVID TIMES

THE QUADCITIES.COM

YEARS PART TWO:

OF TIGER KINGS

AND COVID TIMES

2020

This book is published in the United States by Dreaming World Books and Dreams Reach Productions.

ISBN 978-1-948662-07-9

Library of Congress # Applied for.

Cover photo and design by Sean Leary.

Special thanks to everyone who has helped contribute to the success of QuadCities.com from the time I got there in January 2016 until present day.

It's been a great ride... let's keep enjoying the trip!

As always,

For Jackson

CONTENTS

So, we ready to get this started?

Ok then!

INTRODUCTION

There was no winning Bingo card for 2020.

Nobody had any idea what was going to happen, especially when it all started happening.

The year started routinely enough for all of us. Your typical New Year's Eve celebrations, winter, post-holiday stuff.

There were a few vague stories about some sort of illness going around in China, but hey, weren't there stories every year about some virus going around in some other country on the other side of the planet? Didn't we have other things to think about? Who was going to win the Super Bowl anyway, and what should I put on my New Year's Resolutions list?

Little did I, or any of us, know, but that resolutions list was going to have to be drastically altered. Especially if it involved travel.

By the time February came around, the economy started to take a hit, and the virus started to be taken a little more seriously. But still, we went about our regular lives.

Then, it all came crashing down in mid-March.

The country, and the world, was shut down.

Schools were closed.

Workplaces and businesses were closed.

And we all silently, and perhaps not-so-silently behind closed doors, welcomed it all.

Wow! Here we were able to take some time off! We could sleep in, didn't have to take the kids to school, and we were all working at home so we could set our own schedules. The kids eventually started taking classes online, but, again, the schedules were more flexible and we were all working from home, so it seemed much more laid back.

Everyone was online talking about it, and for a brief time, everyone seemed to kinda get along because we were all in the same boat. It was interesting to see how alleviating some of the stress from the GO-GO-GO!!!! Mentality also brought down the level of acrimony between people in a larger social situation. People seemed to get along better, conversations seemed to go easier, just in that brief time as the pandemic quarantine started to settle in.

We talked about shows we were binge watching, mostly on Netflix, especially one involving this crazy guy called the Tiger King.

Amazingly, some businesses were allowed to remain open, most notably liquor stores, grocery stores, and carry-out and drive-thru restaurants. Which meant that all of us started eating out a whole lot more often, and, as was certainly the case with me, we all started gaining a lot more weight since we were binging on takeout food and lounging around watching Netflix a lot of the time.

Then, things started to take a turn for the worse. Slowly, at first, then far more rapidly.

Covid started to hit people, and hard. People started actually getting hospitalized and dying. Things started to get a little more "real."

The grocery stores started to get dystopian, with shelves emptied of staples, food shelves looking bare, and toilet paper in particular becoming a valuable commodity.

You knew it was bad when packages of Charmin started to be offered at over-inflated prices on Amazon.

People started to get a little freaked out. People added police scanner apps to their phone. People started stockpiling things. Gun sales went way up.

And then the protests started, and the riots, and the discontent, and the people starting to deny and question the covid narrative, and soon, social media went from being a lighthearted place where people discussed the Tiger King to a place where people hated each other and were more divided than ever.

And it was all worse than before, actually, because now people could launch attacks at each other from the comfort of their own couches, because we were all on our own couches.

The year was equally topsy turvy for me, as our advertisers with QuadCities.com had to back off because they were suddenly out of business. We, like so many other businesses, got hit hard, and for about a year I was technically unemployed because we didn't have the money to pay me. Suddenly, I was struggling to get by, and had to really scrimp, save, and make some tough decisions and some creative budgets to make it through.

But I did.

And so did many others in this crazy year.

The irony of it all is that I never did get covid that year, or the following year, when it was at its peak. Nope, I didn't get covid until late in 2022, as it was fading away into something as ubiquitous and banal as the flu.

But for a long time in 2020, we had no idea covid was going to end up that way. We had no idea how much more deadly it was going to get.

Because the pandemic hit the area arts scene so hard, I began covering its impact in-depth and we had to completely change our coverage on QuadCities.com. Whereas before we were pretty much strictly all entertainment and positive news all the time, now we were adding a lot of health coverage and almost daily stories on the new covid numbers, restrictions, and other breaking news.

My diligent coverage of it did pay off for the website. Traffic on the site soared to where we were getting over 100,000 hits a day on some days. And in addition to that, my reporting and writing was recognized on a national level, and twice I was given Google News Awards for my coverage of covid's impact on our area arts scene and the Quad-Cities in general.

It was an honor I would've gladly given away in a second for just a normal, regular year.

But that wasn't to be.

Undoubtedly, we will all remember where we were and what we did during 2020. From covid to riots to the presidential election to the economic collapse to the toilet paper shortages to Tiger King to TikTok and more, it was one of the craziest years any of us could've ever lived through. I can only imagine how my son and other kids are going to look back and remember it in their own lives.

I'm still not sure how to feel about it. It certainly wasn't a great year by any means, and there were myriad challenges throughout.

But then again, I did love spending the extra time with my son, working from home and homeschooling him. I'll always cherish that time.

The columns in this book reflect that up-and-down mood, and reflect the strange and bizarre pop cultural topography and unpredictable world event landscape of that crazy year.

Looking over these columns, here in 2022 as I'm writing this, it seems so long ago. It seems like a different era. But not as different as the era before covid happened. THAT seems like an entirely different world.

To me, it's reminiscent of 9/11. I remember at the time feeling very torn between two extremely distinct points in history. The time before it happened, the freewheeling '90s, and everything after. It seemed as if everything had changed. It seems that way now when I think about the time before covid. This world seems so much different. And, to be honest, not for the better in many ways.

But, it is what it is.

We keep on moving forward.

Unless we're doing a little literary tourism moving back, such as with this book.

Whatever your history, I hope you find it entertaining and worth your time. Thank you for taking the journey with me.

Enjoy the trip,

Sean Leary

WOC's Jim Fisher Deserved

A Better Farewell

Jan. 16, 2020

I was never a big fan of Jim Fisher's show.

I know him personally, but not very well. I was a guest on his show a handful of times (where we would often disagree, on live radio), and when we ran into each other in social situations, we could get along fine as long as we avoided any hot button topics. As a person, a human being, I got along with him alright because we had a fairly superficial small talky interaction.

But I can't say I was ever a fan of his show. It's not just that Jim and I often disagreed on topics and politics, it's that the show, especially in the last decade, went off into a deep end of ridiculousness that made me roll my eyes every time I was in the company of someone who was listening to it, and by proxy, forcing me to hear it.

25

But that said, the world does not revolve around my personal preferences, as much as I would love for it to do so. Different people have different preferences and opinions, to which they are entitled in a society with free speech and a variety of expression. And there were those, to be sure, who loved Fisher's show and will miss it.

I begin my column this way to say that this isn't going to be an obsequious farewell to a person or item of pop culture and media I loved and felt was a vital part of my life.

No, this is a column that's about giving credit where it's due, and being fair in calling out something when it's wrong.

And it was wrong, egregiously wrong, the way "I Heart Radio"*, the owner of WOC, treated Jim Fisher.

Fisher was fired this week, immediately and without warning. Taken off the air, off his afternoon show from 2-5:30, and unceremoniously replaced by a syndicated spewing of bloviating asshat Sean Hannity. The move was part of the new "I Heart Radio"* philosophy, which the company is spinning as a bunch of placating bullshit about "employee dislocation," but which is essentially "let's get rid of anyone local that we have to pay and provide benefits to and replace them with a bunch of syndicated stuff that will cost us considerably less money so that we can jerk off our shareholders and overpay our executives."

And along those lines, they unceremoniously kicked to the curb Fisher, a guy who basically made WOC into what it was and is, a broadcast veteran of 60 years, who started with WOC 40 years ago in 1980 when the station first switched to talk radio. The guy, love him or hate him,

26

helped create and foster the medium in the Quad-Cities and for decades helped define it and carry the brand of the station from the local side. Countless morning shows and other jocks came and went, but there was always Fisher, anchoring the afternoon spot.

For FOUR DECADES.

FOUR.

DECADES.

I was a little kid growing up in Chicago when Fisher started here. Some of you were little kids too. Some of you weren't even born.

But some of you, some of you, remember that time when Fisher first started and ruled the local airwaves with the then-revolutionary format of talk radio. It celebrated its heyday alongside the rise of his career, in the '80s and '90s, before falling off and plateauing in popularity over the last two decades, into its current state of "average listener not only knows who Betty Grable and Errol Flynn were, but probably had a crush on one, or both, of them." But throughout the ups and downs, Fisher shouldered on. Through health issues and personal issues and personnel changes, Fisher shouldered on.

There's a romanticism to that work ethic. One which used to mean something in this country. You go to work. You show up. You give your best. You work hard. You toil through adversity. You take pride in what you do. You do your best for your employer, and, in turn, you're rewarded by them, you're rewarded through that system. You could hear Fisher talk about it often. That American dream. That work ethic. It's something that, regardless of politics, I think a lot of us share, and something that I'm certain a lot of Fisher's audience, many of whom were raised through very different economic times, took pride in and represented.

Jim Fisher, like him or not, certainly did.

And in the end, his reward came nowhere near to fitting his effort. What happened to him in no way shape or form befitted someone of his work ethic, experience and stature. What happened to him was in no way deserved.

Fisher was certainly well into retirement age. And so, it would've been appropriate and considerate for the station, if it needed to let him go, to allow him to do so under the umbrella of retirement. It would've been good for them to give him two weeks, three, maybe, to sign off on his own terms. Have on his favorite guests one last time. Talk about his favorite topics. Actually be behind the microphone, at the station he helped make, helped put on the map, helped continue to succeed, to say goodbye, so his audience could hear his voice one last time, hear him signing off.

I'm absolutely certain that if they'd had the chance, the local management of the station would've allowed him to do that. This move isn't their fault. They're just following orders, doing what they're told they have to do, which is an uncomfortable job for anyone, especially when you have to deliver it to a 40-year veteran.

No, the local folks aren't the ones at fault here. It's the spineless, greedy, cowards of the ironically and Orwellian named "I Heart Radio"* who are to blame. Not just for Fisher, but for the hundreds of other people across the country that they let go this week due to those executives' own decades-long incompetence, greed and cluelessness.

They sat back in their lush offices, and while spinning bullshit press releases about how important "being local" and "the people" are, they looked at their long list of "local people" and all they saw were lines on a ledger.

And after all those decades of hard work. After all that espousing of the importance of showing up, of work ethic, of being rewarded for a hard day's work, after all that time talking about the greatness of the American dream, Jim Fisher woke up to find that that's all it was, and that all he was, was a line on a ledger.

Not to his fans. Not to his listeners in the Quad-Cities. Not to the station that, if it were locally-owned, would've given him the signoff he deserved.

He deserved better.

He deserved a lot better.

And whether you loved him or hated him, after 60 years in the business, after 40 years of putting talk radio and WOC on the map here, you have to admit he definitely earned it.

● ● ● ● ● ● ● ● ● ● ● ● ● ● ● ●slghvl0

WOC Could Be A Ratings Giant If They Go Looking For A Bigger 'Fish'

Jan. 31, 2020

When's the last time you listened to WOC?

How old are you?

If you're somewhere under the age of 65, you probably couldn't remember your answer to that first question.

And if you're somewhere over the age of 65, you probably couldn't remember either, only for a different reason.

I keed! I keed!

In all seriousness though, the audience for local talk radio has been growing older and older over the decades. Most of the shows appeal to a decidedly conservative audience and the demographic for those kinds of shows skews older, and not just in radio. Median age of a Fox News prime time viewer? 68.

Jim Fisher, who was recently let go after 40 years at WOC, was certainly an avatar of those statistics. Fisher was pushing 80 and his audience was in the same demographic.

Fisher was undeniably an extremely divisive figure. After Fisher was let go, I wrote a column saying he deserved to be given a more fitting send-off. In that column I explicitly stated that I wasn't a fan of his show, I just thought, given that he was a 40-year veteran of the station since it switched to talk in 1980, he deserved to be able to say goodbye to his audience and shuffle off to retirement. But judging by the response, you would've thought I had said I thought Ebola was a great thing and should be made into a condiment. The column got TONS of responses on social media and via e-mail and about 80 percent of them were not generous towards Fisher. And by saying they were not generous towards Fisher, I'm being very generous towards Fisher. Most of the responses were pretty damn viciously negative towards him and his show.

That's a big problem when that person is the most identifiable radio personality on your station. And it definitely was reflected in the ratings. WOC was in eighth place in the fall 2019 ratings book, and, looking at their average over the past four ratings periods, they were getting about a 4.5 share of the market.

Which is strange when you look at talk radio nationwide.

If you look at national ratings, talk is booming. It's the number one format across all radio, with 10 percent of the overall audience. Not only that, but if you look at podcasts, which are another form of talk radio in a different sphere, it's doing even better, with 32 percent of people saying they listened to a podcast over the past month according to Edison Research. Online radio? Talk is doing gangbusters there too, and 67 percent of people 12-and-older said they listened to an online radio show over the past month, again, according to Edison.

So if you look at that data, it's pretty clear WOC has been underperforming.

And if you look at even more data, it's pretty clear why.

By far, the biggest demographic of radio listeners is from Generation X. BY. FAR.

In second place? Drum roll please.... MILLENIALS.

Yup, millennials.

According to demographic and ratings company Nielsen, "By generation, radio has the largest reach with Generation X (ages 35-54), with 80.5 million listeners tuning during an average month (97% of the Gen X population). This is followed by Millennials (18-34 year olds), with 71.6 million listeners tuning in monthly (95% of the Millennial population)."

So the top two groups listening to the radio are two groups which rarely if ever would've listened to WOC if you cross-reference their format demographics with the overall listenership demographics.

What station has been the fastest-growing with that audience, to the point where there are several articles like this one out there talking about it?

NPR.

Yup.

Something to think about. Especially when you consider what WOC could, and should, do in the future to revamp its numbers and its audience.

I'm not saying that it wouldn't be a huge change for WOC to switch up their format. But I am saying that it might not be a bad one.

If you look at national numbers and see how strongly talk radio and podcasts are doing with younger demographics, particularly those like Gen X and the Millenials, which both draw heavy advertising dollars, and then you look at local numbers and see that trend isn't manifesting here in the Quad-Cities, it's probably a good idea to shake things up a little bit and see if maybe you can't do something different and do better. After all, you're in eighth place at a 4.5 share, it's not like you're messing around with a 10 or 15 (for perspective, the habitual number one rated station in the Quad-Cities, WLLR, routinely scores about an 18 or 19 share.)

So what, in my humble and oh so wise opinion, should WOC do?

Come up with different talk shows and different styles to appeal to a wider audience. I'm not saying go the complete opposite direction and become Air America, for the very good reason that the vast majority of you out there after reading that are saying to yourselves, "What the hell is Air America?" (Answer: It was a liberal talk radio company that was created to counter-program to conservative radio. It didn't last long.)

33

What they should do is actually try something different. You look at the most popular podcasts and radio shows out there and they're kind of a mix. They're not conservative or liberal. The most popular podcast in terms of reach, by far, is the Joe Rogan Show. Rogan pisses off both liberals and conservatives by having guests on that are both liberal and conservative. If you listen to him, he doesn't really hew to any set side, but, depending on the subject, has opinions that fall on both the liberal and conservative sides of the spectrum.

You know what that sounds like? Most people you and I know. Sure, we all know people that are mega-conservative or mega-liberal, but the vast majority of people hold viewpoints from both sides, and the vast majority of people are smart enough and reasonable enough to want to hear different viewpoints and make up their own mind. For the most part, that's what you get from NPR. That's what you get from most podcasts. And, wow, what shows are gaining in popularity again? Oh yeah, NPR and podcasts.

The other thing you get from most popular shows and podcasts is variety. People want to hear stories, they want to listen to various topics. Look at everyone's social media feed. Sure, you'll get a lot of people that are hardcore all politics all the time, but most people showcase a variety of things – entertainment, music, things about families and cooking and sports. Why not have shows that reflect that? Why not have shows that are driven by interesting personalities talking to interesting people instead of polemic-pushers shouting into the echo chamber?

That's what we've tried to do here on QuadCities.com. If you look at our podcast lineup, it's a wide variety of styles and topics and kinds of shows. If you look at our number-one-rated show, my podcast, QCUncut, it features me talking to a wide variety of people – everyone from artists to musicians to politicians to sports figures to business people and more.

That show reflects my own interests. So do the podcasts I listen to. And as a member of Generation X, the statistics show I'm not alone.

Who knows if WOC's parent company, I Heart Radio, will look at those demographics and consider a move in that direction for their local station. But it wouldn't surprise me.

Nor would it surprise me if it became a success, or at least drove the ratings up a bit and broadened the audience. After all, if you're going to try to catch bigger "fish," you need to look to a bigger pond.

And The REAL Winner Of

The Iowa Caucuses Is...

Feb. 4, 2020

You could tell there was something afowl in Iowa for a while.

The scent of something bold, spicy, hot, was in the air.

It was an original recipe for chaos that turned extra crispy as the night dragged on.

And so it's no surprise, that we at QuadCities.com have unplucked a savory scoop.

And when the national media gazes a popeye on it, they'll be fileting those who have tried to cover it up, probably in panko.

What have they been covering?

That the REAL winner of the Iowa caucuses is …

None other than…

CHICKENZILLA.

That's right.

Chickenzilla.

That half-chicken, half-dinosaur bird of ill repute best known for its starring performances in sketch comedies and films throughout the Quad-Cities in the 2000s, as well as its debauched and hellraising behavior following its rocket to stardom.

Chickenzilla.

Iowa, gaze upon the plate of victory, for it is a delicious irony.

Now, some might say, "Well, wait a minute, I didn't even know Chickenzilla was running for president, let alone as a Democrat!"

To those, we have three very important words:

You.

Are.

High.

Oh, no, wait wait wait, those aren't the words; those are for Illinois voters. Here are the three words for Iowa:

Write.

In.

Ballots.

Yep, that's what's been keeping the results delayed for so long. They've been in shock since last night, when people began showing up saying they were caucusing for Chickenzilla as a write-in candidate.

At first, precinct captains thought they might be drunk.

And, well, some were.

Ok, a lot of them were.

Ok, almost all of them were.

But that didn't stop them from standing by their dinofowl and letting their clucks be heard. And, over the cries for Bernie, Pete, Warren, Biden and others, those clucks were heard, and soon, the Chickenzilla Army were crowing.

Precinct volunteers weren't ready for such an uprising. So, they've been scrambling to get the numbers right, needing to check all of the ballots, to make sure that indeed, Chickenzilla is the winner of the Iowa caucuses.

The word has flown down from the henhouse early today that indeed, Chickenzilla was the surprise winner. Now, it just needs to be officially announced by the media, which, let's face it, will probably cover it up. Probably with flour, egg whites and a secret blend of spices.

But why?

Why would Chickenzilla emerge from its apparent life of luxury on a beach, getting tanned and fit, to battle for the Democratic primary?

It's all part of an old grudge.

A burning rivalry.

One which cannot be unanswered.

One which must be met.

Between a long lineage of chickens…

…and a long line of white-haired men, named Sanders.

And so, it's on.

Chickenzilla vs. Sanders. A battle that's going to get extra spicy.

You know there's more than a Colonel of truth to this.

Jonesy Takes His Final Bow

Feb. 27, 2020

"Hey, have you ever heard the one . . ."

And that's how it would usually begin. With a mischievous grin, a conspiratorial wink, and then that little aside, voiced down as if imparting some ribald secret, which, let's face it, he usually was.

That's how Ed "Jonesy" Jones would greet me pretty much every time I walked in to Circa '21 Dinner Playhouse in downtown Rock Island.

Jonesy shuffled off to that spotlight in the sky on Tuesday, at age 92. He'd been retired from Circa for a few years, since 2014, although he was sorely missed. Jonesy was always one of my favorite elements of the Circa experience, a guy with the spirit and sense of humor of an old vaudevillian acting as doorman for a building straight out of the era.

You'd enter the theater, and Jonesy would be there at the door to greet you, with a smile and a joke, and if he knew you well enough, that joke would be a bit spicier than normal. He had a great laugh and smile and a fantastic sense of humor, and a hell of a personality.

Sometimes he'd be dressed in a costume mirroring the featured performance of the time. Sometimes he'd be clad in a suit and tie. But the two things that were ubiquitous about Jonesy were his smile and his air of always having fun, along with a spirit of a little kid who'd just gotten away with something and was devilishly trying to hide it.

"It's a dream come true," Jonesy once told me about his job as the ambassador for the theater. "People treat me nice, I love the bootleggers, I love the people at Circa. Where can you have more fun, see all the great shows and meet all the people?"

Born June 3, 1927, and growing up a half-hour outside Boston, he got started in theater as a little kid, hitting the spotlight with a self-created sketch, "Jones and Jones," in which he shared the billing with a marionette. In high school, he performed in every show he could, and made it a habit to hit the theaters outside the classrooms as well.

"I've always gone to the theater, I've always had a vivid imagination," Jonesy told me in an interview in 2010 for Get Your Good News.com. "Theater has always attracted me. I've always been like that. I don't know why. My family would go to every show, any musical, any play. I saw Josephine Baker, Maurice Chevalier, all the top stars would come to Boston, and we'd always go to see them. When I was older, I was always on the train to go see shows, Jackie Gleason, Mickey Rooney, there were some great shows there."

After a stint in the army between World War II and Korea, he went to broadcasting school, which is how he ended up in the Quad-Cities. After graduating, he got a job at WOC-TV, spending 25 years working as a director and behind-the-scenes guy.

"It was a lot like theater," he said. "It was black-and-white TV, and there weren't many programs or stations, so we were really kind of flying by the seat of our pants. Most of the stuff we did was live, and oh, it was a lot of fun!"

After broadcasting, he got into a sales company with his wife, selling air and water purification systems. "She proved to be much better at the business than I was," Jonesy said. "So she took it over, and I took on a bunch of different odd jobs."

Jonesy's resume included stints as a night watchman and a pasta chef before he found his true calling.

"I saw an ad for Circa '21, looking for a lobby host, and I thought, that sounds like fun," he said. "I went in and talked to Denny (Hitchcock) and we hit it off and he offered me the job. It's been great. They treat me really well."

And in return, Circa had itself a bona fide character to welcome people to their house of characters. Jonesy was a beloved part of the Circa experience. People would wonder beforehand how he'd be dressed and in which costume if the show had a theme that suited it, and he would work with costumer Greg Hiatt to come up with appropriate and humorous garb. Every once in a while, he'd be a part of one of the shows, and would come up to the stage for a one-liner or two. But usually, he'd greet you with a wide grin and lead you to your seat, making small talk and throwing out jokes along the way. It was an incredibly charming detail that made the Circa experience special and one-of-a-kind, just like Jonesy.

"This is a dream job," he said of Circa. "Where else can I stand backstage and talk to Tony Bennett or trade jokes with the Smothers Brothers? I feel like I'm a kid again. This is what I always dreamed of."

I knew Ed beyond the realm of Circa as well. Jonesy's humor could also be seen in a number of short and feature films I wrote and directed with My Verona Productions. He had cameo roles in "Your Favorite Band," "The Return of Taco" and "Dingo Boogaloo," among others. In each, he delivered his lines with panache and sly humor, cracking up myself, my producing partner Tristan Tapscott, and everyone on the set. He was always a fantastic character, always such a vibrant personality, always just so much damn fun to work with.

"Those were a lot of fun to do," Jonesy said in that 2010 interview. "It's always fun to do comedy, to make people laugh. That's what it's all about. Life is to be enjoyed. You're only put on this earth for so long, so you've got to enjoy it. That's what I'm doing. I'm lucky enough to be doing what I love, and I have been for a long time. I've led a wonderful life."

He did. And he met his final curtain in similar style. According to his obituary, he died surrounded by his family, and one of the last things he said to Jeannie with a big smile was, "I love you and thanks for 65 years together and all the trips taken with the kids."

He was beloved by the local theater family, and we thank him for all of the journeys we embarked upon with him, the jokes told, the laughter and smiles. Jonesy truly was one of a kind. He will be missed.

Laura Fraembs' Legacy Is One Of Hard Work And Journalistic Integrity

March 31, 2020

Laura Fraembs wasn't well-known to the general public outside of local media circles.

She wasn't on TV, or radio, and her picture rarely appeared in the newspapers for which she'd worked since 1981, The Dispatch and Rock Island Argus, and then the Quad City Times.

In fact, she hated attention and shied away from the spotlight.

But Fraembs' legacy of integrity and veracity, absolutely spartan work ethic, and dedication to the principles of journalism, made her a true star of local media and an irreplaceable part of the newspapers.

I was very sad to hear about her passing away way-too-early at age 60 last week after injuries sustained from a fall in her home. Laura and I worked together during the entire time I was at the Rock Island Argus and Dispatch, and then again at the Times after the papers merged, and she was one of my direct editors, along with Joe Payne, when I was with the Illinois-side papers.

Laura was a terrific editor, one of the hardest workers I've ever seen and someone who was very direct, pragmatic, and did not tolerate BS. I always respected and appreciated that about her. In an era of the often phony, in a business increasingly strewn with artifice and compromise, she was always direct, always to the point, always genuine. You always knew where you stood with her, and that was something I loved and admired about her.

We didn't always agree, since I was, and am, very hard-headed, stubborn, creatively passionate and oftentimes a gigantic pain in the ass. But as was often the case, that conflict produced excellent work. When we clashed, it was because we both wanted the best, both wanted to be the best, but had different opinions on how to get there. The answer was usually somewhere in the mix of the two, and I appreciated the fact that she saw things differently from me, stood her ground with equal stubbornness, and helped me to see that perspective and strive to achieve the greatest goal. I know many times Joe and Laura had to deal with me being a frustrating, obdurate, rebellious, titanic SOB, and many times, as much as I stubbornly didn't want to admit it, they were right. And I appreciate that. Their passionate devotion to us doing our best made me a better writer, reporter and person.

At all times, Laura was fiercely independent, amazingly strong, devoted, absolutely relentless in her work ethic and unabashedly dedicated to doing her best. She was never one of the "local media celebrities," but she was far more valuable, she was one of the people who made sure the papers adhered to a code of quality and ethics that maintained a vital veracity.

She was also incredibly funny, snarky, sarcastic, and fun to talk to, especially when shooting the bull outside during breaks. She had a terrific laugh, and a fantastic way of cutting through the crap to deliver a great sarcastic line, which was usually well on target in terms of its subject.

There is no replacing a Laura Fraembs. There is no replacing someone who constantly worked the longest hours of anyone there, who always went that proverbial extra mile. With her it wasn't a cliche. It was legit. She was the one who would stick around to get it right, to make sure it was done to the best of her ability, to make sure it was at its best before it went out to the readers. It didn't matter how long she'd already been there, or what she had going on after work, that wasn't just her job, it was her vocation, and that was vital to her. It was inspiring to see, and not something you see often. I admired and respected the hell out of her for it.

The newsroom will have a massive void in her departure. You don't just find another Laura Fraembs.

The lives of her friends, family, and longtime boyfriend, Kurt, who was the perfect lighthearted comedic complement to Laura, will also feel her departure heavily. My condolences go out to them. She'll live on in the warm and kind memories we all have of her, as well as the incredible integrity and quality she brought to local journalism.

There will never be another Laura Fraembs. She will most definitely be missed.

Advice To My Son Is Good

Advice For Life

April 4, 2020

My son Jackson turned twelve this week. He is undeniably
the best person I've ever had the honor of meeting, and I'm
looking forward to continuing to experience the adventure
of his life with him.

And as that time goes by, he may ask me for the advice I've
gained in my years before him and since he's been born.

That's why I started writing this list of things I've learned
and I wish my parents had told me.

I started it shortly after he was born, and I've added to it
and published it every year on his birthday since, and, now,
I've published it in a book, called, shockingly enough,
Advice To My Son.

As I look at the list, it's good advice for me to follow as well.

And, in thinking about the times we're living in right now, it's just good advice in general.

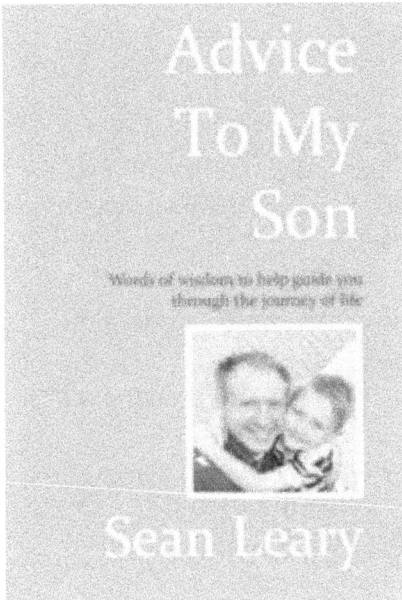

Here are some of the important things I've tried to impart upon him:

A friend is someone who is with you when you have nothing to offer them but your friendship.

Remember the people who are with you when you're down. They're the only ones who deserve to be with you when you're up.

It's never a bad thing to be a good, respectful person. In the end, you're the one who has to look at yourself in the mirror, and if you can say you did the right thing, you'll always be able to do that and smile.

Always keep an open mind, until you need to close it.

People will show you who they are, if you let them, and you have the patience to observe. The question is, do you want to see people as they really are, or do you want to see them as you want them to be, using the shorthand of what they reveal with your imagination and desires for what you wish them to be filling the gaps?

You aren't what you say you are, you are what you do.

Anyone can destroy, but it takes a greater person to create.

If anyone ever asks you what you want to be when you grow up, tell them you want to be happy. If you're happy, everything else just kind of falls into place.

Someday, someone is going to break your heart. It will tear you apart. It will make you feel awful. But somehow, somehow, try to retain the thought that this, too, is a positive thing. You're not meant to be with them if they don't want to be with you. And by leaving you, they're giving you an important gift – the freedom to potentially find the person with whom you ARE meant to be.

What do you look for in a significant other? Someone who makes you happy as much as possible, because life's too short and your time is too important to be with someone who makes you unhappy more often than not. Someone who makes you proud of yourself and your actions when you're with them. Someone who you're proud to be with.

Someone who brings out your best, but stands by you at your worst. Always remember, you don't have to be with anyone to be happy or complete. You can be happy all by yourself. So choose carefully, and pick someone who is going to add to your life, who is going to make it a better place far more often than not.

When you're going out on a date, remember these things: Be nice, be polite, be yourself.

Someday, you may find yourself in a difficult part of life, going through some hardship. You may look back at previous times in your life when things were much better. The pessimist is going to think "Look at how much better things were. I'll never be that happy again." The optimist is going to think "Look at how much better things were. If I was that happy before, I can be that happy again." Always be the optimist. Life changes, circumstances change, but as long as your faith in yourself remains the same, and as long as you move forward and make positive decisions, you can always get your life back on track.

While going through those difficult times, always remember that there are things you can control, and things you can't control. Worry about the things you can control, and always try to do your best in making them better. One thing you can always control is your thoughts. Try to make them happy ones – think of things that make you laugh, jokes, friends, happy memories with people you love, like your Daddy. Those will make you smile and laugh and once you're smiling and laughing, no matter what, your life is going to be at least a little bit better.

Always keep a treasure chest of happy memories, jokes, funny movie scenes or funny things in your head that you can always turn to when you need a laugh. Whenever things aren't going great, pull stuff out of that treasure chest, think of those funny jokes and good times. And whenever you experience something that makes you laugh or makes you smile a lot, file it away in that treasure chest. It'll be the best investment you ever made.

If someone treats you bad, more often than not, it's because of them instead of you. If you treat people politely and with respect, and they treat you badly, you have nothing to feel bad about. Don't waste your time with those people.

It takes a while to eschew the security of labels, until you realize labels hold no security. Everything from wedding vows on down has been broken and discarded, worthless. The only way to know if something is sure and true is if you both realize your life would be profoundly diminished due to the absence of the other, and that there's no one with whom you could imagine spending your time and having as much joy and love in your life.

The strongest bonds are forged when traveling on narrow paths.

Sometimes things aren't too good to be true, they're just good and true.

Really, when it comes down to it, you either see your life as a miracle or an accident. You won't find out whether you're correct until you die, but your answer will go a long way in determining your happiness while you're alive.

Criticism is just someone else's opinion. Just like yours.

If you can make yourself laugh, you'll never be completely unhappy.

The best gift you can give yourself is your own love and friendship. You are a wonderful person and you have every right to be happy with yourself. If you can be, then you'll never truly be alone. You'll always have yourself to keep you company.

Always remember at least one really funny movie quote. One line that never fails to make you laugh or smile when you remember it. You'll need it when you're at your most down, to remind you that life brings laughter as well.

Along the same line, always have at least one really wonderful memory to hold on to, to cherish, and to remind you of the beautiful things in life, and that no matter how sad you might be at any given time, life has the potential to bring great happiness too. I hope I've given you enough of those good memories to last a lifetime.

The best way to say you're sorry is to consider your actions before you commit to them and decide not to do hurtful things in the first place, so you won't have to apologize later.

Good things can happen to anyone. But first you have to believe they can happen to you.

It's always better to be hated for what you are than loved for what you are not.

Life isn't about finding yourself, it's about creating yourself.

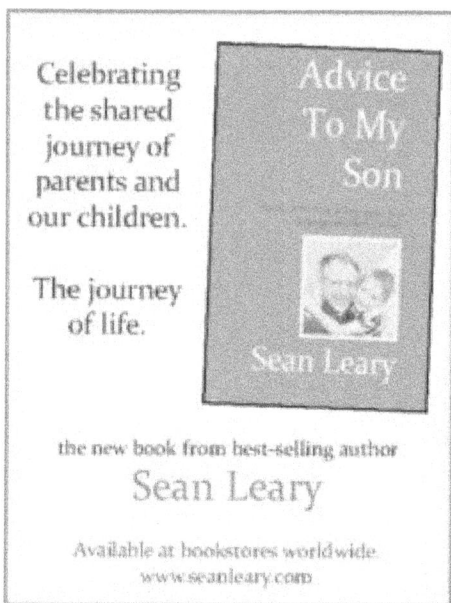

There are some people in life that are always optimistic, no matter what, and some people that are always pessimistic, no matter what. Always make sure that you surround yourself with as many of the former as possible. It'll make all the difference.

Always make sure you have plenty of creative people in your life. You'll never want for surprises.

Don't be afraid to believe the good things people say about you. It may always seem easier for the bad things to stick, but both are opinions, so why not allow the good ones greater weight?

Friends are people who make your life better for being in it. If they don't, and what's more, if they consistently make your life the worse for being a part of it, they're not worth having in your life. There are six billion people in this world. You can find better friends. You don't need anyone who brings you down and isn't worthy of you — or even more important, who isn't worthy of the person you want to be.

The same goes for the person with whom you're in a relationship. They should make you a better person for them being in your life, and you should do the same.

Every day when you look in the mirror take time to notice your positive attributes. Concentrate on them. Celebrate them. Allow them to take greater prominence than those negative things you may feel the self-defeating need to dwell upon. Life is too short for you to make yourself unhappy.

It's not "mean" or "selfish" to retain some self-worth and expect appreciation and reciprocation. You are a valuable person. You are an important person. You are worthwhile. Don't forget that, or allow anyone to convince you otherwise.

Never underestimate the power of discipline and perseverance. The difference between those who accomplish things and those who talk for years about wanting to accomplish them, but who never do, is that the former know how to translate words into action and maintain their direction in doing so, regardless of the inevitable obstacles that come their way.

Consider the ramifications of your decisions. Every decision, big and small, sets you on a path. It sends you towards one thing and away from another. Often, the larger the decision, the bigger the sacrifice of other options. So if you're going to choose one thing over another, be damn sure that the thing you're choosing is worth it, and will be in the long run.

Whenever you get advice, consider the source. People's worldviews and attitudes tend to impinge upon their opinions. If someone is in an optimistic state, they'll tend to give good and upbeat advice, and will tend to be more supportive of positive actions you might be taking. If they're in a pessimistic state, they'll tend to be more negative and cynical about both positive and negative actions. Take all advice, but keep that in mind and add as many grains of salt as needed accordingly if someone with a pessimistic slant always seems to be shooting you down without good reason.

The journey of 1,000 miles doesn't begin with a single step. It begins with the thought and the conviction that you are going to take that step.

No matter what you do or where you go I'll always be thinking of you. No matter how old you get, I'll always remember you as the tiny blessing you were the day you were born. And no matter what, I'll always love you.

And that's love: When you're always there for someone, and you always want to be.

'What Kind Of Music Do You Like?' Is Kind Of A Loaded Question

April 22, 2020

What kind of music do you like?

Who are your favorite singers?

What's your favorite song?

When I was younger, particularly in high school and early college, I was inclined to judge potential friends and girlfriends in large part on their musical and pop-culture tastes.

Yes, I was an entertainment snob.

Hard to believe, I know.

It was always kind of a loaded question, and sometimes a question to ask when you were loaded, but it tended to have grand implications for the way I would look at that person going forward, in a way perhaps small and insignificant, or a way much more significant. It all depended on the answer. I'm not saying this was right, I am not saying this was the most mature or educated or emotionally evolved way to go about assessing my compatibility with people. But, I am admitting that I was biased. (Note: Was. Past tense. I'm more mature and forgiving now. Mostly.)

In comparing preferences in music, TV shows, movies and books, I felt you could tell a lot about how much you would have in common in other areas. Each of my favorites reveals a defining trait about me. An idealism. An ideal. A passion. A way of looking at the world. A way I work, a way my mind and heart moves.

To some extent, this is still true. As I think it is for most people. Look at someone's list of favorite books, TV shows or music, and you learn a lot about that person. Certainly this may seem superficial, but then again, so is basing attraction solely on each other's physical attributes, and that definitely hasn't gone out of favor.

But what if there's something more to this? What if a person's inner workings, chemistry and physiological proclivities actually are revealed by these things?

Stick with me here.

We, as human beings, are in our essence a series of molecules that are mostly empty space. If you look at an atom, it's a tiny nucleus surrounded by protons and electrons that are once again, quite small. In between those solid bodies? Nothingness.

So what holds us together?

Movement. Vibration.

Our atoms vibrate at a set rate that makes us solid. This is science. It's proven. And likewise, it's also been proven that certain vibratory states or exposure to certain sonic sensations elicit certain physical reactions. It could be something as simple as a pounding bass driving us to the dance floor or something as complex as the military firing microwave pulses toward an oncoming army to cause headaches.

So if this reaction to vibration unites us, if our bodies are so entwined with these vibrations, wouldn't it make sense that those of us who react strongly to certain vibrations — i.e., musical styles — would share a certain body chemistry or rate of vibration that produces a similar reaction?

And likewise, couldn't that be transferred to literature, which is a series of words, symbols for sounds that likewise create similar vibrations either internally or externally?

And if we share a certain vibratory state, wouldn't it stand to reason that we might share other similiar physiological and psychological (by way of physiological) traits?

Ergo, we would have more in common.

So, maybe it's not so far-fetched to think that if you and another person have very similar musical or literary tastes, you may have more in common with that person on a deeper, quantum physics, atomic kind of level.

Just something to think about the next time you're on a date and someone asks you what kind of music or books you like . . .

Dirtying Up Soap Operas In The Time Of Covid

May 7, 2020

Over the last week, or several, I've been home, unable to do much but sit around on the couch and watch TV. In between catching up on the shows I'd TiVo'ed ages ago ("Barry" was excellent, BTW), I stopped by to sample a few minutes of daytime TV shows and soap operas.

It's pretty funny in a goofy way, catching up on the amazing, Dickensian plotlines being brought to life by over-actors on a daily basis. After all, how many other stories do I read that feature the names Bianca, Ridge and Alcazar?

Even more entertaining are the plot rundowns of the soaps.

Some of the descriptions are fairly standard country song fare (she left me and done me wrong) or Springeresque stuff (she left me and done me wrong for both my brother and his wife, who then had a sex change to satisfy her), but some are a little more adventurous. Some include vampires that done left werewolves and done them wrong.

Actually though, I wish there were even more bizarre soaps. If I was in charge of writing some of them, I think the descriptions might look a little more like this…

As The Quarantine Continues: Everyone wondered why Poopy wasn't wearing a mask and several people shunned and criticized him online for it. The "Candelabra Killer" stalked Rika but she was saved when Tito gave her a ride on his Segway as the inspirational music of Night Ranger played in the background. Later, while out maiming Englishmen on the moors and investigating the "Candelabra Murders," Jak the werewolf discovered an incriminating ruffled shirt and pompador wig at Sebastian's bistro. Pumpkin tried to convince Paris that Jones wasn't her baby and was actually an alien from the planet Sheeshk, but Paris became vexed and wouldn't believe her. Later, while Paris was in a post-hypnotic trance brought on by extraterrestrial messages relayed through the "Montel" show, Jones ordered a Galactic Gunshorr to eliminate the earthling Pumpkin.

As The Delivery Driver Stands Outside: Carly was impressed that Steve remembered her favorite pizza toppings. Juicy asked if the driver had brought extra napkins because the store was out of toilet paper. Binaca flew into a murderous rage when Trucker returned from the store with Sierra Mist rather than Sprite. Trog and Fiesta discovered a rare strain of human DNA that may or may not explain the disappearance of the harelipped quadruplets at Corby Ridge, then, to celebrate, they made love.

All My Real Children: Dylan threw his binky when his Mommy turned off Barney. Porky ate all the melon, Bunky had none and Peachy cried all the way home. Jordan and Jeremy have each grown three full inches in the last year! Cremora announced, via bumper sticker, that she was the proud parent of an Honor Student at Plunger Way Junior High. Jebby Jethro announced, via bumper sticker, that Calvin doesn't like Jeff Gordon. Paige wondered whether it was a good idea to feed a baby chili.

I Can't Believe Those People: Several people shopping at Walmart scratched themselves in unseemly places and the videos went viral. After a nuclear confrontation in the Ti-D-Mart parking lot, Cusack proposed a duel with Zabka over the affections of Beth, who has secretly been cheating on both of them with Donger. Regis discovered Diego was a zombie. Alfie tried to break Kitana out of the clutches of the Noonatics, a cult led by former Hermans Hermits lead singer Peter Noone.

The Passions Of Netflix Binging: Carole killed her husband and fed him to tigers. Joe brought in four new husbands. Julian was interviewed by Carson after "Art Is All" went to the top of the charts, and on live TV gave all his love to a shocked Martin. Kingpin (the dwarf) trashed Possumburger's house after discovering he had been having an affair with Schmoovia. Kingpin (the giant) had his plans for world domination through a race of super-ghouls decimated when that adorable scamp, Jinkies, accidentally tripped on the cord and disconnected the super-ghouls' suspended animation chambers from the electro-generator. To make matters worse, Jinkies taped an episode of "Lizzie McGuire" over Kingpin's ransom tape, which he planned to send to the leaders of the free world. Oh, Jinkies, you so wack!

The Bold And The Beautiful: Dondeesta learned that Forquita was pregnant with the vampire Rich Nice's baby. After realizing Taj and Jubbles slept together, Porcupine threatened Taj and told him he would ruin his ketchup-flavored chip business. Jim wished he had a more exciting name.

Days Of Our Lives: Deacon was fired because he was a total bush. Psy was strangled by Beauregard but managed to get free from the dungeon and went into hiding in South America, where Rocky taught him the ways of the ninja. Rush admitted he was addicted to painkillers, but continued to rip the same liberal drug policies that allowed him to escape jail time. Remembering those hot summer nights on Fire Island, Big Bubba salivated at the prospect of Rush actually spending time in jail, then went back to creating a shiv out of a toothbrush for the big gang war/cotillion ball scheduled at Worship's Brick Penitentiary later that evening.

General Hospital: Ira said his goiter had been bothering him. Alcatraz complained of a bloated feeling after winning the mustard-eating contest. Xandria reported she had lost a gerbil. Nikandra and Mechagodzilla began to rain terror and destruction down on the hospital, which had been magically transported through a time warp to Tokyo by Wantigo, who was jealous of Chinastra (Pookie) for making love to Joanie. Ziggy played guitar.

The Young And The Restless: Nicolai and Penelope developed a special water/air combination mattress specifically designed for the needs of the young, restless sleeper. The end of the world was averted when Sanders was able to find the mystic Ferrari pendant and use its touch to defeat Sears (Serge Menken). Charisma and Alyson had a Jell-O-wrestling competition to save the sick kids.

The Writer On The Deadline: Sean finished his column.

Why Are 'Tiger King' And 'Last Dance' So Popular During Covid?

May 18, 2020

It's been said there are no coincidences.

All actions, all events, are part of a lattice of connection that perhaps we can't see, and of which we're not aware, but that we all feel, consciously or unconsciously.

That's what it means when you say something feels right. It feels like it should be. It feels like it should be of our time.

That seems to be true especially when it comes to entertainment. To be sure, at all times, there is popular entertainment. There is always something moving through the transom of our lives, of our consciousness, taking up the spotlight. But there are so few of those avatars of popular culture which become truly transcendent, that go beyond mere popularity to become not just ubiquitous but somehow perfectly fitting for that particular time. The Beatles. Nirvana. Reality TV. TikTok.

It's why the two most resonant programs during the covid-19 pandemic have been "Tiger King" and "The Last Dance."

On the surface, they couldn't be more disparate.

"Tiger King" was garish and lurid, the tale of seedy and strange zookeepers, rivals who no one could really root for, but who captivated our attention with their sensationalistic and selfish battles while behind-the-scenes, the alleged reason for their being, the tigers, were abused and used as props for their power plays.

"The Last Dance," on the other hand, was bittersweet, beautiful and nostalgic, the story of one of the greatest athletes in the history of sports, and the way his farewell was tainted, ending an era in a sad and regretful way that still feels like an open scar.

Both of them have mesmerized viewers like no other shows during the past two months.

And when you look at the last two months, it's no wonder why.

The time of covid has been chaotic and difficult, unprecedented in all of our lifetimes. It's left people completely confused and feeling a strange sense of unease, because we have no reference point to it. None of us were alive and cogent during the last true pandemic over 100 years ago, and even if we were, the times have changed so much it would almost be irrelevant as to how each has impacted society.

Wars, recessions, political attacks, social violence, environmental disasters, those, sadly, have been mapped for us, and, also, sadly, we've become almost used to them, we take them in stride. However, this is new territory. We've never seen this particular virus because it's something new, we've also never had a pandemic shut down governments and economies so thoroughly or have something we couldn't truly control or get a handle on have such an impact on society. We also haven't had anything like this happen during a time when people were all online and the spread of disinformation and the feeling of not knowing who or what to believe was so pervasive. It's left people feeling very uncertain and adrift.

And so, whether consciously or subconsciously, we seek some stability to bear this time out.

Most of us had no choice but to weather it inside, and most of us turned to our televisions for escape and subconscious catharsis.

And that's why "Tiger King" and "The Last Dance" have been so popular, because they've been so relevant to that catharsis.

"Tiger King" came at the beginning of the pandemic, when everything was chaotic and unknown. We had no idea how to deal with this new normal. It was bizarre and unwieldy and, for many, frightening. We had no bearing to navigate it.

And in the midst of the frenzy emerged this show, which was completely chaotic and bizarre and unwieldy and, underneath its oddity, perverse and frightening, dealing with killing and violence and bloodshed.

But through watching it, we could escape. Not just in terms of entertainment and vicarious thrills, but through using it as a conduit for all the uncertainty and chaos of that early part of the quarantine.

Through all the chaos of "Tiger King," there was humor, there was levity, there was some sense of being able to step outside the turbulence and stand watch as it happened to someone else, and in being able to do so, it made us feel better about ourselves and our worlds. Subconsciously, perhaps, it was a way of laughing through fear and uncertainty. But there was also something that struck a familiar chord for us. In many ways, we were the tigers, the ostensible reason for being for this world, watching as our leaders from various sides squabbled, fought, grasped for power, and trafficked in the ridiculous and audacious, all while we were left to just wait and see how this circus was going to affect our well-being. We had little to no control over it, so at best all we could do was laugh at the absurdity and chaos of everything. "Tiger King" gave us an outlet for that.

Eventually, however, things somewhat stabilized. We began to embrace the new normal. It became easier for us to get by, to navigate the strangeness of the new world, with all of the social distancing and masks and working from home and everything else that went along with it.

But along with acceptance and assimilation came an air of sadness.

Came a recognition of loss.

Once we were able to navigate our new world, once we were able to get beyond the initial shock – the fight or flight mechanism that honed our attention to only that which was pertinent to the here and now – we were able to think, to feel, about what was happening.

And that wasn't necessarily a good feeling.

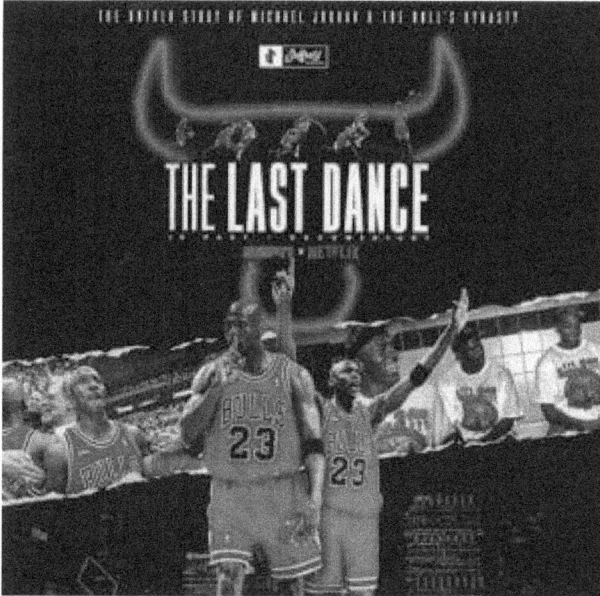

We thought about the missed graduations, and birthdays, and sports seasons, and our friends and family, and just our normal lives and being able to do things we'd always taken for granted.

We were surviving, we were navigating it, yes, but it wasn't our ideal. It wasn't what we wanted.

And that's where "The Last Dance" came in.

When was the last time things were truly good for us and our country?

74

The '90s.

Before 9/11. Before the endless wars. Before the umpteen recessions and economic collapses. Before the bloodthirsty divisiveness and hatred between sides. The virulent tribalism of the internet. The superficiality and insecurity fomented by social media and reality TV. The constant "scandals" pushed to goose media ratings. The huge economic divides.

The '90s were, for most of us, the last time things seemed good, or even seemed like they had the hope of being good, beyond any cynicism.

The Chicago Bulls of the '90s and Michael Jordan represented that idyll. They were the prominent sports and pop culture heroes of our time. Watching that show reminds us of where we were then, and who we were then, both as individuals, and as a nation.

The economy was great. We weren't at war. We certainly weren't in quarantine. The cost of living, the cost of college, the cost of everything, was far lower. And while there were definitely political and social divisions, as there have been for centuries, they weren't anywhere as vicious as now, and they weren't being flamed by the ubiquity of opinions on social media. It was a pre-9/11 world. And it was a pre-ubiquitous internet world, where the new technology we were just learning about was full of nothing but hope for a better future, a better time, a better life for all of us.

Watching "The Last Dance" isn't just about watching the Chicago Bulls. It's about taking a time machine back to a time when things were so much easier and simpler. The last time we could actually, truly, say that.

And, like "The Last Dance," like the end of those Chicago Bulls and Jordan's career, it feels like it ended far too soon, and was taken away from us long before our time, by forces beyond our control.

And we miss it. We miss having that hope, that opportunity, that world that seemed so much easier to navigate.

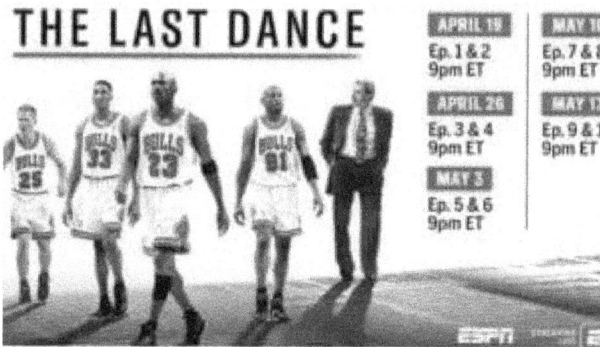

THE LAST DANCE

And in watching Michael Jordan, one of the greatest athletes in the history of any sport, a man who worked relentlessly, with incredible loyalty, to build not just himself but his organization, from nothing, many of us feel some sense of community with him. We think of the years of our lives spent poured into hard work, unpaid overtime, incredible loyalty, to companies and businesses and a way of life, only to see it rewarded with job loss, a lack of appreciation, and a venomous condescending arrogance. When Jordan spits out Jerry Krause's line about "organizations winning championships" being used to dismantle one of the greatest teams ever, he's not just speaking for the Bulls, he's speaking for all of us who have seen offices full of great, hard-working people at the tops of their games get capriciously and cruelly cut away.

It's always difficult during times like these. It's often impossible for many of us to express our feelings, to put them into words, or even fully express that we even feel them. But they're there. And oftentimes, whether consciously or not, we seek out entertainment, alleged escapism, in the form of some catharsis, that allows us to watch and experience these things and to get those feelings out through the characters on screen, through the things going on in these movies and shows.

When nobody knew what to expect, when everything was a surprise, when we desperately wanted to be able to laugh in the face of fear and the potential of something horrible, "Tiger King" was there, giving us constant surprises that we could laugh at and that entertained us, and an underlying tone of terror that we could experience with distance and a dark humor, like the catharsis of a horror film.

And as we came to grips with that, as we began to really mourn and feel the bittersweet nature of life during covid, there was "The Last Dance," to allow us to feel those same things through the people in the film, somehow wishing they could go back, for one last dance with that era, and yet knowing they could only look back and wonder, and hope that someday, things would be right again.

The same way we are now. Wondering. Uncertain. Hoping that someday, things will be right again.

That's the role entertainment plays for us.

That's how it touches our souls, our hearts.

That's why it's important to us.

And that's why it's been so important to us during this time. Because we've needed it now, more than ever. And we still do.

Be Considerate Of Service Workers During The Rush To Re-Open

June 8, 2020

Well, fingers crossed, this past weekend began the grand re-opening of society after the covid quarantine. In some states, like Illinois, we're not entirely 100 percent back to normal, but it's certainly stepping in that direction. On the Iowa side, it's full boar, all in, back to the way it was, and, again, fingers crossed that we stay that way.

People are squirrelly and jacked up like spider monkeys on Mountain Dew after months of being in lockdown on social distancing protocols, and as such, it's probably going to be a wild couple of weeks. But, as always, it's important to be considerate and positive towards those people who are going to be taking the brunt of this enthusiasm — service workers, especially those in food service and bar work.

A friend of mine recently shared an item on Facebook that I felt summed up my feelings quite well, and I'd like to share it with you, regarding a code of conduct during this time to remain considerate to those working in food and bar service. It's been going around Facebook, so I'm not sure who to credit for it, so, whoever you are out there, well-stated and well-done.

What's it say? Well, here ya go…

READ THIS before you decide to dine out:

Yes! Restaurant patios will be open ! This is a new world though. You're most likely going to a restaurant that threw together a patio in hopes of making some money. The building was not designed for this. They are trying their best but everything may not be perfect. Eating in the streets is fun but it's going to be hard on the employees. They have to wear a mask and gloves no matter how hot and go possibly a few hundred feet to get more water. They are going to be hot, sweaty and most likely overwhelmed because these restaurants are not set up for this. Please help your servers in this journey by doing the following:

1. Don't run your server. Try your best to ask for everything you need at once. Remember it's going to be a long walk from the street into the building for more water or anything else. Help us out by asking all at once

Radicle Effect Brewerks in Rock Island was one of many businesses to re-open to the public this past weekend.

2. No mask jokes or your views on them. The server has to wear it. They have no choice and really your opinion of them while you're eating not wearing one means nothing to them.

3. The server is wearing the mask to protect you and you have nothing on to protect them. Wash your hands.

4. You eat. You go. Eat your meal. Have some drinks but please do not sit at a table all night unless you continue to spend money. These restaurants are working with very limited space. They can't afford for you to order 2 side salads and water and sit there 4 hours. Yes people do do that. All the time.

5. Don't come out if you are sick.

6. Social distancing. Keep yourselves at your own table. Be aware of the rules.

7. Cut everyone some slack. Everything may be a bit slow because this is basically a new job for everyone. Be kind.

8. Tip. They are going to be hot and sweating and it's hard to breathe wearing masks all to make a buck. Please treat them right and leave a decent tip. If you can't afford to tip you can't afford to go out.

9. Be pleasant. You should be happy. You're finally out.

10. Realize that the staff is doing their best.

11. Remember you have 3 meals a day every day of your life. This is only one of them. Calm down and enjoy it!

11a. Please re-read #8. Many people in this industry have been out of work for a while. While you are being happy to be out of the house, remember this and be generous.

When Will Summer Concerts And Big Venue Shows Return

June 12, 2020

For many, this will be their first summer without an outdoor concert.

The first year in a long time without a festival.

The first stretch without them going to see their favorite artist.

When will we turn that around and get to see those touring acts, get to go to those big concerts and shows?

We have no idea.

Cautious optimism. That's the best description of where we're at right now in regard to the covid-19 situation and its impact on not just the Quad-Cities arts scene, but the economy of the entire country, especially in regard to live performances, and most particularly in regard to touring acts.

Iowa Governor Kim Reynolds lifted a vast number of restrictions today, allowing all businesses to re-open, albeit with some social distancing protocols intact.

Illinois remains in an even more restrictive state of caution, with some businesses still not allowed to open and those that are allowed being placed under the same social distancing protocols.

By many metrics, these precautions are working. Numbers in New York City and Chicago, two of the hardest hit areas, are falling. So there is good news to report, and that's obviously a beacon during a time that's still been extremely difficult and tragic for many – especially those who work in the arts industry, which has been absolutely devastated by covid-19.

There have been few industries hit as hard as the arts. Performing arts venues, like Moline's TaxSlayer Center, Davenport's Adler Theater, and East Moline's Rust Belt, have had to wipe their slate clean, and have no accurate timetable to open. We've seen some shows, such as Smashing Pumpkins' sold-out gig at Rust Belt, go from rescheduled, to postponed, to canceled. That's reflecting the uncertainty of the times, and, also reflecting the fact that the touring acts ultimately control when they decide to go back out and when the shows are going to go on.

Some fans were pissed at The Rust Belt, and made fun of them for changing it so many times, but it's not the fault of the folks at The Rust Belt, who would've loved to have had the show. Ultimately, the decision is the performer's as to when they're going to go on tour, and during a time of uncertainty such as this, you can't really blame the performers either. They have massive crews and expenses to deal with and it's a risk for them as well, financially, aside from the health concerns.

Which leads to the next question: Even if the TaxSlayer, Adler or Rust Belt wanted to open, who are they going to book? Most acts have canceled their tours at least through the summer, some through the rest of the year. And, even if many of them opened tomorrow, they would need to have enough of a slate of shows to justify their financial output. If only 30 percent of acts are back out touring, is booking names from that 30 percent going to bring in enough money to offset the costs of throwing the shows?

All of those venues employ hundreds of people. They make up an intricate web of cooperation behind-the-scenes to ensure that the show that you and your friends go to see comes off without a hitch. We seldom acknowledge just how many people go into the spectacle because if they do their jobs right, the event is seamless. But the employment of all those people is an expensive venture, and it requires booking acts who are going to sell tickets and concessions to pay for those employees.

Sadly, the lack of these venues means those employees – everyone from tech folks to security to concession workers and more — remain without that income. Those people aren't just numbers, they're human beings, with families, with bills, with the stressors of having to find income that isn't there anymore. It's easy for someone to say, "Oh well, just go on unemployment," but anyone who's actually been on unemployment realizes it's not as easy as a facile, glib comment. There are far more complications and uncertainties. There are limitations. And those people are still having to deal with that.

The local theater, club and restaurant scene has been even harder hit, putting out not just those workers, but the owners and managers of those venues in profound ways. The TaxSlayer, Adler, and Rust Belt have the benefit of at least partial help from the community coffers and don't have to worry about closing their doors any time soon. Independent businesses who also depend on touring performers, like Circa '21, RIBCO and the like do not.

Some, which are not-for-profit, are fortunate enough to receive grant money from public and private organizations, but it's hardly a fortune, and still leaves them skating on the edge.

Those that are privately owned, and for-profit entities, like Circa, or RIBCO, are in a far more tenuous position, having to fall back on reserves and whatever relief they can get from the meager covid stimulus bill Washington deigned to pass.

And even after other businesses are allowed to open, slowly, the arts organizations will still be last in line to recover, because they make their money on large crowds, which are exactly what the preventative measures are designed to avoid. When will that arrive? Nobody knows.

As I previously mentioned, in some cases – New York City, Chicago, some states – it's getting better, fueling an optimism that we're getting beyond the curve.

But by many metrics it's getting worse. A number of states are seeing spikes in numbers. Arizona, South Carolina, Florida, Alaska, Arkansas, California, Kentucky, New Mexico, North Carolina, Mississippi, Oregon, Tennessee, Texas, Utah and Puerto Rico have all seen spikes. How long and how dramatic those spikes will be is unknown.

When it comes to local businesses impacted by the availability of national performers, that matters. It's one thing for some of the states to be doing well, and that's definitely great news, especially for businesses that are locally-based and thrive utilizing a regional distribution model for their products and a local model for their audience.

However, when your business model is dependent upon performers coming in from out of town, and there remains a sharp inconsistency in the cases and effect of covid along those pathways, it makes it heavily problematic for those businesses.

Some could potentially evolve beyond that. Circa and other theaters could eschew bringing in national actors and showcase regional and local performers, at least in the short term. Local clubs like RIBCO could showcase more local and regional bands. There could be slow opens for both, involving social distancing strata to start, and then evolving towards the old normal as cases subside, with the hope that people will feel secure in going out again and experiencing life as we knew it.

However, it's going to be far longer for places like TaxSlayer, Adler and Rust Belt, not to mention any other larger performing venues and outdoor concerts and festivals. It's not just whether or not the audiences will arrive, it's also a matter of employees and staffing, financial considerations, and in being able to book acts who are actually out on tour. When will that happen? This fall? This winter? Next spring? Next summer? Nobody really knows.

Cautious optimism.

That's where we're at right now, as the first steps start to be taken.

Be safe. Be smart. Be careful.

And maybe, hopefully, this will be the last summer season without concerts we'll see for a long while.

Good Things To Remember

On Father's Day, And

Every Day, With Your

Children

June 21, 2020

Time is the only thing you can spend once.

As we go into Father's Day weekend, that's something to definitely remember. Being a father, bringing another life into the world, is an amazing experience and responsibility, and it gives you a blessing in time to spend with a person who will always be a part of your life, and who is beholden to you for helping to shape them as a person. You can literally make the world a better place by making the time

89

and effort to make your children better people. To be there for them. To enjoy your time with them. To be a parent and friend to help guide them through the world.

A friend of mine recently became a Dad, again, and is going through his third round of changing diapers, 3 a.m. feedings, and the constant care and diligence that goes into being a parent. We were talking about that, and, like myself, when I was in the same situation, he sees even those chores as something to cherish, something to remember, because that time flies by quickly. And those moments are accompanied by so much change — first steps, first words, first smiles and laughs and jokes, those firsts are something that can't be replicated, can only be enjoyed once if you're there for them.

On February 2, 2009, in the midst of the last big recession, I was laid off my full-time job as entertainment editor for three newspapers. Within a few weeks, my part-time jobs, as entertainment correspondent for six radio stations and two TV stations, were gone as well. It was a stressful time, financially. But I was also happy.

The life of a journalist is not easy. There are a lot of long hours. When I was with the newspapers and other media outlets, 12 hour days were routine. The last few months of my tenure, it was into work by 9, and I'd maybe get home by 8 p.m. Maybe, if I didn't have a concert to review or something to cover at night. Oh, and I'd often have to work weekend nights if there was something going on that needed to be covered.

My son was 10 months old at the time, and I didn't want to be reviewing Foghat at the fair when he took his first steps, said his first words. So I completely rearranged the paradigm of my life. I started freelancing, working from home as much as possible, so I could control my schedule and spend as much time with him as possible. It meant making a lot of sacrifices, getting rid of the nicer car and going with one more affordable, not going out to eat as much, not spending as frivolously, but it was well worth it for the time I would get to spend with my son. As a result, I was there when he took his first step. I heard his first words and sentences. Got to teach him his letters and numbers, draw his first pictures with him, teach him how to play soccer, and basketball, and baseball. Got to get to know him as a human being, as his own person, and got to be there to help guide him in becoming a human being and evolving and growing through this world.

He is undeniably the best person I've ever had the honor of meeting, and I'm looking forward to experiencing the adventure of his life with him. And as that time goes by, he may ask me for the advice I've gained in my years before him. Which is why I started writing this list shortly after he was born, and I've added to it and published it every year on his birthday since. I eventually turned it into a book, Advice To My Son. I still add to the list, to give to him every year, on his birthday and Father's Day, which is a holiday we share.

And as I look at some of the items on the list, it's good advice for me to follow as well. I hope you find it helpful as well.

A friend is someone who is with you when you have nothing to offer them but your friendship.

Remember the people who are with you when you're down. They're the only ones who deserve to be with you when you're up.

It's never a bad thing to be a good, respectful person. In the end, you're the one who has to look at yourself in the mirror, and if you can say you did the right thing, you'll always be able to do that and smile.

Always keep an open mind, until you need to close it.

People will show you who they are, if you let them, and you have the patience to observe. The question is, do you want to see people as they really are, or do you want to see them as you want them to be, using the shorthand of what they reveal with your imagination and desires for what you wish them to be filling the gaps?

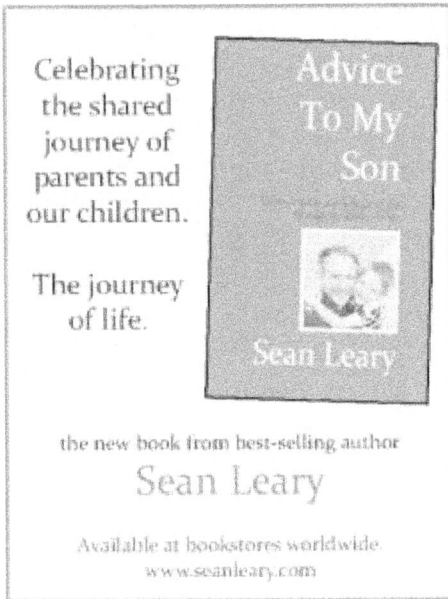

You aren't what you say you are, you are what you do.

Anyone can destroy, but it takes a greater person to create.

If anyone ever asks you what you want to be when you grow up, tell them you want to be happy. If you're happy, everything else just kind of falls into place.

Someday, someone is going to break your heart. It will tear you apart. It will make you feel awful. But somehow, somehow, try to retain the thought that this, too, is a positive thing. You're not meant to be with them if they don't want to be with you. And by leaving you, they're giving you an important gift – the freedom to potentially find the person with whom you ARE meant to be.

What do you look for in a partner? Someone who makes you happy as much as possible, because life's too short and your time is too important to be with someone who makes you unhappy more often than not. Someone who makes you proud of yourself and your actions when you're with them. Someone who you're proud to be with. Someone who brings out your best, but stands by you at your worst. Always remember, you don't have to be with anyone to be happy or complete. You can be happy all by yourself. So choose carefully, and pick someone who is going to add to your life, who is going to make it a better place far more often than not.

When you're going out on a date, remember these things: Be nice, be polite, be yourself.

Someday, you may find yourself in a difficult part of life, going through some hardship. You may look back at previous times in your life when things were much better. The pessimist is going to think "Look at how much better things were. I'll never be that happy again." The optimist is going to think "Look at how much better things were. If I was that happy before, I can be that happy again." Always be the optimist. Life changes, circumstances change, but as long as your faith in yourself remains the same, and as long as you move forward and make positive decisions, you can always get your life back on track.

While going through those difficult times, always remember that there are things you can control, and things you can't control. Worry about the things you can control, and always try to do your best in making them better. One thing you can always control is your thoughts. Try to make them happy ones – think of things that make you laugh, jokes, friends, happy memories with people you love, like your Dad. Those will make you smile and laugh and once you're smiling and laughing, no matter what, your life is going to be at least a little bit better.

94

Always keep a treasure chest of happy memories, jokes, funny movie scenes or funny things in your head that you can always turn to when you need a laugh. Whenever things aren't going great, pull stuff out of that treasure chest, think of those funny jokes and good times. And whenever you experience something that makes you laugh or makes you smile a lot, file it away in that treasure chest. It'll be the best investment you ever made.

If someone treats you bad, more often than not, it's because of them instead of you. If you treat people politely and with respect, and they treat you badly, you have nothing to feel bad about. Don't waste your time with those people.

The strongest bonds are forged when traveling on narrow paths.

Sometimes things aren't too good to be true, they're just good and true.

Really, when it comes down to it, you either see your life as a miracle or an accident. You won't find out whether you're correct until you die, but your answer will go a long way in determining your happiness while you're alive.

Criticism is just someone else's opinion. Just like yours.

If you can make yourself laugh, you'll never be completely unhappy.

The best gift you can give yourself is your own love and friendship. You are a wonderful person and you have every right to be happy with yourself. If you can be, then you'll never truly be alone. You'll always have yourself to keep you company.

Always remember at least one really funny movie quote. One line that never fails to make you laugh or smile when you remember it. You'll need it when you're at your most down, to remind you that life brings laughter as well.

Along the same line, always have at least one really wonderful memory to hold on to, to cherish, and to remind you of the beautiful things in life, and that no matter how sad you might be at any given time, life has the potential to bring great happiness too. I hope I've given you enough of those good memories to last a lifetime.

The best way to say you're sorry is to consider your actions before you commit to them and decide not to do hurtful things in the first place, so you won't have to apologize later.

Good things can happen to anyone. But first you have to believe they can happen to you.

It's always better to be hated for what you are than loved for what you are not.

There are some people in life that are always optimistic, no matter what, and some people that are always pessimistic, no matter what. Always make sure that you surround yourself with as many of the former as possible. It'll make all the difference.

Always make sure you have plenty of creative people in your life. You'll never want for surprises.

Don't be afraid to believe the good things people say about you. It may always seem easier for the bad things to stick, but both are opinions, so why not allow the good ones greater weight?

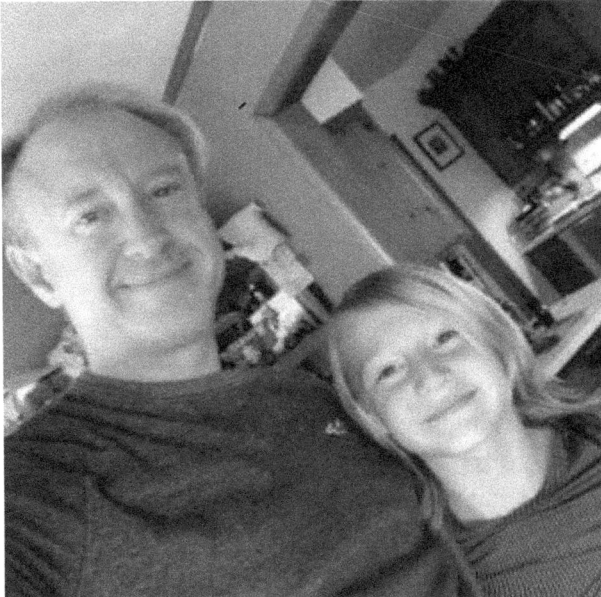

Friends are people who make your life better for being in it. If they don't, and what's more, if they consistently make your life the worse for being a part of it, they're not worth having in your life. There are six billion people in this world. You can find better friends. You don't need anyone who brings you down and isn't worthy of you — or even more important, who isn't worthy of the person you want to be.

The same goes for the person with whom you're in a relationship. They should make you a better person for them being in your life, and you should do the same.

Every day when you look in the mirror take time to notice your positive attributes. Concentrate on them. Celebrate them. Allow them to take greater prominence than those negative things you may feel the self-defeating need to dwell upon. Life is too short for you to make yourself unhappy.

It's not "mean" or "selfish" to retain some self-worth and expect appreciation and reciprocation. You are a valuable person. You are an important person. You are worthwhile. Don't forget that, or allow anyone to convince you otherwise.

Never underestimate the power of discipline and perseverance. The difference between those who accomplish things and those who talk for years about wanting to accomplish them, but who never do, is that the former know how to translate words into action and maintain their direction in doing so, regardless of the inevitable obstacles that come their way.

Consider the ramifications of your decisions. Every decision, big and small, sets you on a path. It sends you towards one thing and away from another. Often, the larger the decision, the bigger the sacrifice of other options. So if you're going to choose one thing over another, be damn sure that the thing you're choosing is worth it, and will be in the long run.

Whenever you get advice, consider the source. People's worldviews and attitudes tend to impinge upon their opinions. If someone is in an optimistic state, they'll tend to give more good and upbeat advice, and will tend to be more supportive of positive actions you might be taking. If they're in a pessimistic state, they'll tend to be more negative and cynical about both positive and negative actions. Take all advice, but keep that in mind and add as many grains of salt as needed accordingly if someone with a pessimistic slant always seems to be shooting you down without good reason.

The journey of 1,000 miles doesn't begin with a single step. It begins with the thought and the conviction that you are going to take that step.

No matter what you do or where you go I'll always be thinking of you. No matter how old you get, I'll always remember you as the tiny blessing you were the day you were born. And no matter what, I'll always love you.

And that's love: When you're always there for someone, and you always want to be.

Can You Become Addicted

To Videogames?

June 26, 2020

"Fortnite."

"Overwatch."

"God Of War."

Know anyone who plays those games?

Know people who say, or demonstrate by their actions, that they're "addicted" to those games?

Think they're exaggerating?

They might not be.

It sounds like a sci-fi scenario, but from a logical standpoint, you could become addicted to video games.

Much like anything else addicting, all it would require would be repetitive stimulation of the right portions of the brain, creating a psychological and physiological need.

And given the practice of playing video games, that's not so far-fetched.

All video games are a sequence of pre-programmed reactions to your actions.

Your actions are accompanied by a series of synapses firing in your brain, creating connections between your actions, your emotions, the chemicals released into your cerebral cortex, and the visual stimuli before you that is leading to your reactions.

Ergo, as you embark upon playing a video game, you are being programmed. Your brain is firing in a certain pattern the same way the game's computer chips are firing against that pattern in an attempt to elude you and beat you.

But in the meantime, certain areas of your brain are being consistently stimulated. Over. And over.

So, say a computer company wanted to get you hooked on a video game.

It would look at research into the pleasure and addictive centers of the brain and create a game that stimulates those areas on a consistent enough basis that you finally go beyond the breaking point and develop an "addiction" to that game.

But … what if the scientific proof of the potency of that addiction was also able to be manipulated for other means?

What if the video-game companies began selling "ad space" — placing subliminal messages in games at points past that threshold of addiction and suggestibility? Since your brain would be more open to that suggestion and addiction, it would be easier for, say, fast-food companies or soda manufacturers to get compliant gamers hooked on their products without them even realizing it. Their conscious minds would be so occupied with the games that their subconscious would be defenseless, and thereby more easily programmed.

So, for example, after an hour or two of playing "Overwatch," suddenly, inexplicably, you would develop an intense craving for Taco Bell or Mountain Dew. Which would seem really odd. Especially if you were a vegetarian on a strict macrobiotic diet.

And if you can program people to buy more fast food or energy drinks or shoes or video games or whatever, what if you could program them to participate in other, more provocative behaviors?

What if, after a certain number of hours of attempting to master a game, a player would reach a threshold of stimulation that would realign his cerebral chemistry to get him to think a certain way, support a certain position, or generally be more fearful or suspicious or insecure? Which could, in turn, open him up to more suggestions to purchase certain products that addressed those nascent needs?

Of course, the programming wouldn't have much of an effect on the casual gamer. However, the person who spends hours and hours or entire days in front of a gaming screen would find himself an unwitting vessel.

Addicted to video games?

That could be the least of his concerns.

Now if you'll excuse me, I need to finish my burrito loco, Red Bull and this game of Fortnite.

Quad-Cities Hit With A King-Sized Departure From The Local Arts Scene

July 3, 2020

Few people outside the small local comedy community realized that Andrew King moved away from the Quad-Cities this month.

Few people outside the small local comedy community know who Andrew King is.

But the departure of the soon-to-be-30-year-old King, who finally made a long covid-postponed move to Providence, R.I. in late June, is a real creative diminishment to the local arts scene.

King was one of the most original characters on the Quad-Cities entertainment scene. He brought a unique voice, persona and artistic vision to the local stage. With an asymmetrical poof of hair, bookish glasses, and a predilection to wearing vintage sportscoats adorned with funky little buttons, he looked like the geeky, pagan offspring of a gene melding of Woody Allen, Elvis Costello and another Quad-Cities original, Scott Morschhauser.

And like Morschhauser, who blazed his own singular path across local entertainment with bands like The Kabalas and The Metrolites, before completely taking himself off the map and retiring from performance in 2009, King is going to be missed for his ideas and energy that lent an offbeat patina to the mural of local entertainment.

King arrived on the local scene about a decade ago, with the Blacklist Comedy Troupe, but after realizing the loud stomp of raucous improv didn't jibe with the silence and clever thought bubbles of his more jazzy vocal beats, he transitioned to stand-up, and began to develop his own voice and persona.

The After Hour logo, by local artist Johnnie Cluney

Influenced by an eclectic mix of comics and TV shows, from Garry Shandling to "The Dick Cavett Show" to Tom Snyder and Steve Allen, with a little bit of Hawkeye from "M.A.S.H." thrown in, King found his niche with the inception of his live talk shows, beginning with Rozz Talk, at Rock Island's Rozz Tox.

It was a pretty simple formula – King on stage, much like any other live talk show of the past or present, most notably Tom Snyder's "Tomorrow," with one guest, having a conversation. It's a formula which had been done before – I had done it, Kai Swanson had done it, Don Wooten had done it – but one which hadn't been done in a while, and King brought his own unique persona to the equation to make it new again.

He really hit his stride with the offshoot project of that, The After Hour, which had its home at the Circa '21 Speakeasy, and was, for a brief time, a companion show with my own sketch comedy at the Speakeasy, "Rock City Live." The After Hour was a brilliant creation. It was, in all

ways, a live talk show no different than those of Kimmel or Fallon, with its own set, desk, and guests, from comedians to musicians. Whereas some people, again, including yours truly, had done similar things in the past, no one did it to this extent, with this attention to detail and setting. It was fantastic to see, and one of the greatest things to hit the local arts scene over the last decade, in my opinion. What made it all the more intriguing to me was that King was such a huge fan of the masterpiece, "The Larry Sanders Show," and so much of his inspiration and persona was influenced by that brilliant meta-comedy. As with all of his work, it added an extra dimension of smarts and cleverness to his comedy and his creation.

Andrew King caricature by local artist Metro Catpiss

The same could be said for his other signature project, The Bix Beiderbomb Open Mic Night, which had much in common with many other open mic nights past and present, but, again, with King emceeing and handling the odd and quirky promotion of it, took on a distinct life and spin of its own.

And that's what I'll miss about Andrew King being a part of the Quad-Cities arts scene. Like all great artists, he could take something that had been done before, that could've been banal or mundane, and instead gave it a twist, a weird new direction, something that was distinct to his own vision, that made it new and interesting.

That vibrance is always needed in an arts and entertainment scene to make it vital, to make it not just commercially successful, but artistically successful.

I have no doubt King is going to succeed in the Providence, and, ultimately, Boston, environment, which will offer him a much larger and urbane audience for his work. The arcane references, inside jokes and little details, the influences and sparks, will resonate with a bigger crowd in a bigger market. I'm happy for him, I'll be glad to see him succeed.

And, I'll be glad to see him periodically return, just for a visit or a performance, to the area.

But it's also sad to watch him go. It's unfortunate for the local arts scene to see a funny and active creative mind leave the area. He'll be missed.

Best of luck, my friend.

You may now flip.

● ● ● ● ● ● ● ● ● ● ● ● ● ● ● ●slghvl0

Forget Kanye, I Am Formally Announcing My Campaign For President

July 10, 2020

Ok, so about 50 percent of you hate Donald Trump.

And, about 50 percent of you hate Joe Biden.

But, probably about 90 percent of you, whether you like his music or not, think Kanye West is pretty freaking insane.

This week, Ye, as the kids like to call him, was more crazy like a fox with the brilliant public relations stunt of announcing he's going to run for president.

Never mind that he hasn't formally filed to run, and never mind that he's way past the deadline to do so or be on the

110

ballot in a vast majority of states, so technically, he has no chance. The fact that he announced it at all was absolute genius on his part, because the actual campaign of running for president wasn't what this was all about, it was about the attention he's gotten and will get for announcing a campaign.

Say what you want about Kanye, but he is masterful at manipulating the media and generating tons of attention for himself. Even if it is often under the adage of "no press is bad press," because, let's face it, he routinely gets his share of bad press.

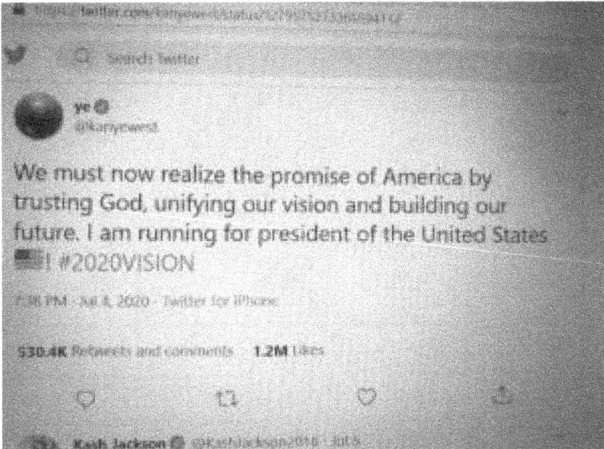

But I'm actually kind of amused by Kanye and his goofy stunts, including this one. As we watch as the mainstream media actually gives this ridiculous publicity grab credence by going to the point of even arguing whether Kanye might tip the election to Trump or Biden by siphoning off part of the vote, Kanye just continues to get more time in the limelight. Good for him!

And, good for me!

Because, in the spirit of Kanye West, I'd like to formally announce that I AM RUNNING FOR PRESIDENT OF THE UNITED STATES OF AMERICA.

That's right. Never mind that I haven't filed or that it's past the deadline in several states. Never mind that I'm not especially well known outside the Quad-Cities and some snippets around Chicago and Southern California. All that matters is that I AM ANNOUNCING FORMALLY THAT I'M RUNNING FOR PRESIDENT OF THE UNITED STATES OF AMERICA.

Now, let me state right away that this has nothing to do with me trying to sell copies of my books, which you can get locally at The Book Rack and online at Amazon.com and a variety of other online booksellers. While you may really enjoy my best-selling collection of short stories, Every Number Is Lucky To Someone, which was nominated for an Oprah's Book Club pick, or my science-fiction novel, Black Knight Apocalypse, which Diana Gabaldon, author of the Outlander series called "Very imaginative," or even my children's book with my son, Jackson, Here Comes The Goot!, or, let's say my fantasy series, The Arimathean, which asks the question, what if the three wise men were ninja wizards sent to protect Jesus from being killed by the Satan-possessed King Herod?, I insist that I'm not just making this presidential announcement to sell my books! Not even my new novel, due in stores worldwide August 8, called Subliminal Cartography, which has been described by critics as "a brilliant cross between 'Magnolia' and 'The Royal Tenenbaums.'"

No, I'm running for president to make some incredibly important changes to this country, because we're a country of dreamers and doers, of people of action and accomplishment, who get things done, who love our freedom and our country, who are humble people who value hard work and commitment, and that's why if I'm elected, I'll be MAKING AMERICA KICK MORE ASS THAN EVER, DAMN IT!

So, how am I going to do that?

Glad I'm imagining that millions of you are asking, let alone giving a crap, because otherwise I'd have to think of another idea for a column this week!

Now, of course, I'm not going to be revealing ALL of my agenda at this point, or even my vice president (The Rock) but there are a few things that I will be doing as president that you will be thrilled to read about. Such as:

- During these troubling times of covid and unemployment, I will be making Netflix, Hulu and Disney Plus FREE for all American households. That's right, FREE, honchos! So, how am I going to do this? Partially through a system of tax breaks and other incentives for the companies that own them, and partially through a "bullshit tax." Anyone who shares a Facebook meme that is blatantly bullshit will automatically be taxed two cents, appropriately enough, because they're giving their two cents. Although after my tax is implemented their two cents will actually benefit people and people will actually give a fiddlers fap about it. Economists and social observers estimate this should generate several trillion dollars per year, not only paying for my free Netflix, Hulu and Disney plan, but also helping to pay for ...
- The This One's On The House Plan, in which every week, drones will deliver a slate of fresh drinks to every American over the age of 18. (Must be 21 or over to claim alcoholic drinks.) Want Starbucks? Some wine

from Binnys? Root beer from A&W? You got it! This will be paid for by the previous tax and also a special tax on anyone who blames their ridiculous behavior or decisions on their Astrological sign. Mix and match 'em, you'll get a sixer of whatever you want, courtesy of my tax on people who blame their horrible yet entertaining dating decisions and woeful drama-fest friendships on the fact that they're a Sagittarius. (It's only six drinks per week, because Sunday is a day of rest, ya friggin' alcoholics.)

- In addition to overhauling the immigration policies in a humane, productive and common sense way, I will reallocate all monies previously allocated to the useless border wall to creating an America-wide Taco Tuesday. Every Tuesday, two free tacos for everyone! This will be paid for by taxing everyone who shares that Facebook status about them taking control of all your photos tomorrow if you don't share that status. Also, just to show Canada that we love them too, we will create Donuts And Bacon Wednesday, Eh? That will be paid for by taxing anyone who hashtags or uses the phrases "I can't even" or "living my best life," or any dude who posts a picture to a dating profile in which he's shirtless or holding a fish. (Jesus, I'll probably balance the budget on that one alone! Get ready for prosperity, America!)

- All Confederate statues will be replaced by statues of Burt Reynolds as The Bandit, Ludacris, Outkast, or Waffle Houses. All represent a celebration of Southern culture and history in different ways, without being freakin' racist. Statues of Burt Reynolds' mustache are also acceptable. This will be paid for by taxing all guys who begin text conversations with women with "hey." Every "hey" will be taxed, to, ahem, make hay for the treasury. (I'll pause for a moment while you laugh uncontrollably at that joke.)

-

- "The Star Spangled Banner" will no longer be the National Anthem, and will be replaced by "Party in the U.S.A.," by Miley Cyrus, because it's a beautiful ode to everyone in America overcoming their differences and divides by joining together to, yes, yes, Party in the U.S.A. (Lone tear slowly falls down my cheek as I smile in pride.) Runner up: "Born To Run," by Bruce Springsteen. Considered but disqualified due to the band being British: "Pour Some Sugar On Me," by Def Leppard.
- I will not ask to be addressed as Mr. President, but rather, as Batman. "You magnificent bastard" is also acceptable, as is "O Captain, my captain!" and "Mike Honcho."
- I will continue the grand tradition of an open and free press and hold many press conferences, but before I will answer any questions from members of the media they will first have to answer a trivia question about "Beverly Hills 90210." I also promise that at least in every other press conference, one of the trivia questions will be about Muntz.
- Any company calling itself an American company and taking advantage of American tax incentives must move its operations and jobs back to America and as much as possible purchase its products from American companies or it must preface the name of said company with the phrase Poopy Diaper UnAmerican Rat Bastard (insert company name here). Yes, I'm looking at you, Poopy Diaper UnAmerican Rat Bastard WalMart.
- I will order the United States Treasury to begin creating a special new bill, the 1999 dollar bill, featuring a picture of Prince on the front, and Morris Day and The Time on the back.
- Taylor Swift will be allowed to finish 2020 with her VMA Award, but must turn it over to Beyonce in 2021.

Admittedly, the last one is a blatant attempt to court Kanye voters.

So there you have it – Leary 2020, MAKING AMERICA KICK MORE ASS THAN EVER, DAMN IT!*

It's Time To Go Down The Rabbit Hole Of S-Anon

July 17, 2020

Listen, I'm not going to say that Kanye West dropped out of the race for President of the United States just because I announced I was running.

After all, I'm writing this, not reading it out loud.

But I do find it coincidental that after I announced I was running for president last Friday, within days, Kanye suddenly dropped his 2020 campaign.

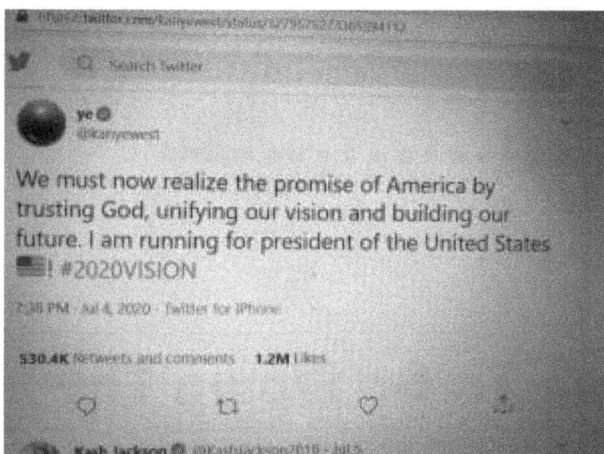

ye 🌀
@kanyewest

We must now realize the promise of America by trusting God, unifying our vision and building our future. I am running for president of the United States 🇺🇸! #2020VISION

7:38 PM · Jul 4, 2020 · Twitter for iPhone

530.4K Retweets and comments   1.2M Likes

Kash Jackson 🌀 @KashJackson2018 · Jul 5

Hmmm.

Suspicious.

Kind of like a lot of other behavior by famous folks lately.

Perhaps you've been hearing about some of it. Certain big-name celebrities have been shockingly AWOL the past few months.

Tom Hanks.

Ellen DeGeneres.

Pauly Shore.

All of these huge stars and more – Jimmy Kimmel, Oprah, Steven Spielberg, Gary Coleman, Harry Potter (if he existed), the Quaker Oats guy, etc. – have been dubiously off the radar for most of this year.

Now, some people who have been "brainwashed by the corporate media" (i.e. people with common sense and other

118

things to worry about; significant others that they prefer to have sex with rather than spend time on the internet; lives, etc.) might say that they haven't been seen because of the covid pandemic shutting down most of the entertainment world. Especially Pauly Shore. And the Quaker Oats guy.

But those "sheeple" don't know what they're talking about.

According to a clandestine group of internet warriors, all of these disappearances have been tied to a mysterious and insidious conspiracy called Q-Anon.

Now, for those of you unaware of Q-Anon (i.e. people with common sense and other things to worry about; sex lives, etc.), it's a popular conspiracy theory that's been sweeping the Interwebs.

According to the theory, hundreds, maybe thousands, of celebrities are part of a secret cult of pedophile devil-worshippers running Hollywood. Allegedly these celebrities have finally been caught and are being brought to justice for their crimes and are all currently under house arrest, which is why they haven't been seen in public that often. They're also allegedly lying and saying that they're in quarantine for covid, but in reality, they're under house arrest for their terrible crimes. Friggin liars.

Those people include Tom Hanks, Oprah, Ellen DeGeneres, Steven Spielberg, Will Smith, Flo from Progressive, Big Ter, Jake from State Farm, Taco, Caillou, and more.

Especially Caillou.

Q-Anon is a heroic anonymous figure on the inside who has discovered all of this and, with the help of his trusty sidekick Donald Trump (no, seriously, I'm not making this up), is helping to destroy the cabal and throw the criminals – including celebrities like Lady Elaine Fairchild, Dora The Explorer, the polliwog from Gullah Gullah Island, Hillary Clinton, and Wilfred Brimley – into jail.

Well, not to be outdone, I've been working towards similar ends, under the code name S-Anon, with many of the same celebrities, to condemn them for their horrible crimes against humanity.

We'll start with Tom Hanks, who has jammed his work with occult symbolism, giving away his demonic leanings. After all, here's a guy who got kinky on national television and spanked twin demons on the buttocks while being dressed up as a sorcerer named "David S. Pumpkins." While many might think the S. stands, blatantly, for Satan, it's a little-known secret that the S. is actually short for "Sssssss," which is the sound a snake makes, and in the

Bible, the devil shows up as a snake. SEE, PEOPLE!!! THESE EVIL CULTS ARE MUCH MORE SUBTLE THAN THAT! You've got to look BEYOND the obvious things like Hanks being in movies called "Inferno" and "Angels and Demons" and instead look to the devious symbolism and undercurrents in his other movies, like "Bachelor Party," which stars a guy named Nick the Dick, who, I learned, is NOT a detective.

This man is evil.

For example, Hanks also once starred in "Sleepless in Seattle," which seemed like it was about a lonely guy looking for love, but was really about a Seattle late night radio host being terrorized by a man afraid of the fact that he was a werewolf who was also in a grunge band; "Philadelphia," which was actually about a haunted philly cheesesteak sandwich which would give people severe indigestion and GERD symptoms; and "Joe Vs. The Volcano," which was actually about a secret society named J.O.E. (I don't think it stood for anything, they just thought it seemed cooler like that) which was trying to take over the world through the hoax of climate change and fake volcano eruptions to bring about a one world government.

Ellen, well, for the past several years, she's been making celebrities come out and dance on her show, and as the good people of the town in "Footloose" can tell you, dancing gets you nowhere but hell. Also, Ellen once starred in a movie called "The Love Letter," which was about a love letter she wrote to none other than the devil on the side of the box of the candy Red Hots. Now, some people (SHEEPLE) might look at that letter and say that it's nothing more than an ode to a sweet little cinnamon candy with just the right amount of zing, but I think we know better, that it's all code for her amore for Beezlebub.

As for Oprah, it's a little known fact that there's been a secret code in all of her book club selections and if you decipher it just the right way, it says "Live, Laugh, Love Satan." In addition, she also introduced the world to the twin necromancers Dr. Oz (symbolic of the Wizard of Oz, which was about a rich elite who used a demonic entity to control the land of Oz), and Dr. Phil (symbolic of the Magician of Phil, which was about a nebbish named Phil who lived with his grandma and had a cape that smelled like Ben Gay and who did shows down at the Elk's Lodge using a magic kit he got in the mail from Doug Henning. He tried to grow out a mustache and afro like Henning but he just couldn't pull it off, and his magic career went nowhere. So he became a serial killer! And now you know… THE REST OF THE STORY), and gave her audience free cars, which we all know cause several accidents each year and contribute to global warming. Nice job, OPRAH!

And then, there's Maude.

AND THEN THERE'S MAUDE.

Satan.

And those are just the tip of the iceberg. As Q and S have discovered and uncovered, the corruption runs very deep in this nationwide, nay, worldwide, web of evil. And only through our diligent efforts, along with our faithful companions Kanye West and Donald Trump, can we root it out, bring it to light, and throw it in jail to blaze a bright new path of goodness and light in our world! It's only through cutting off all the tendrils of this beast that we'll finally be able to get to the head, the core of all the world's evil, the one demonic source of all terrible things in this world, which needs to be eradicated in order for us to bring the earth to salvation and a bright new era.

You know that evil.

You know that darkness.

You know that most sinister being which needs to be eradicated.

Yes.

Of course, I'm talking about Caillou.

Give Credit Where It's Due

July 24, 2020

I want to give kudos to Rein Razer. In our story earlier this week on QuadCities.com on her upcoming burlesque show, Rein Razer's Court of Royalty, coming to Village Theater tonight, she said the following:

"I got the idea from how the Speakeasy was doing their booking for shows."

Seems simple, right? Just actually acknowledging that you got the idea for something from someone else on the local arts scene. But you'd be surprised at how little this is done. More often, much more often, people have an incredible selective amnesia about things others in the scene are doing, even if they've been involved with the exact things they're emulating, and rarely give credit where it's due.

Rein Razer

Listen, it doesn't diminish you and your efforts to acknowledge that you've been inspired by or have gained experience and information from something someone else has done. We're all inspired by others, we all gain experience from looking at the works of others. And it's not only the right thing to do to acknowledge that, but it helps to build the entire scene up, instead of creating unnecessary annoyances.

 I'm the first to admit that when I first moved out here to the Quads, I was inspired by my good friend, Linda Cook. When I moved out here from Chicago, where I'd grown up and gone to college, in the mid- '90s, she was the Entertainment Editor for the Quad City Times, and she was

EVERYWHERE — on Paula Sands Live, on WQPT, on a ton of radio stations, etc., and the former entertainment editors for the Dispatch/Argus had been NOWHERE — neither Bill McElwain nor Eileen Young had ever been regulars on any other local media.

When I took over as Entertainment Editor for the Dispatch, Leader and Rock Island Argus, I was the youngest person in the history of the company to become an editor, so I already had plenty of people doubting and discounting me, and I had to work hard to catch up to the high bar Linda set. And so, as her erstwhile competition at the time, I needed to ramp up my game and try to get out there to promote my own newspaper. Before long, I was all over TV and radio as well, on Paula Sands, the channel 8 morning show, WQPT, a half-dozen radio stations, etc. But it was Linda Cook who spurred me to do that, and at times, she was even generous enough to offer me advice and work with me in that electronic media arena. Her successor, David Burke, likewise became a friend, and as my new competition post-Linda kept the bar high to keep me on my toes and working hard. I'm thankful to both of them.

 I've also frequently admitted that Matthew Clemens was a huge influence on me starting up my own publishing company. After I'd had a few sour experiences with other publishing companies in the '90s and didn't like how they packaged and marketed my work, and also didn't like that they didn't pay out royalties on time and sometimes not at all, Matthew said to me, "Well, why don't you do it yourself?" and pointed me in the right direction. Before long, I was publishing my own work — and the work of many other talented area authors — and I very much enjoyed having full creative control over the design, marketing, etc. of my books, and allowing other authors that same freedom. But that wouldn't have happened if not for my friend Matthew Clemens sending me on that pathway.

The opening scene to the My Verona Productions feature film "Your Favorite Band," with me, right, and Tristan Tapscott.

I also give credit to my frequent artistic collaborators during my years as a film and theater producer/director/etc. — Tristan Tapscott, Scott Beck and Bryan Woods, who helped to bring my ideas and productions to life. Film and theater production is a daunting task, with tons of late nights and a lot of work that often goes sorely uncompensated other than in artistic satisfaction. Working with Tristan, Scott and Bryan on the various My Verona Productions shows we did together from 2003-2007 was a blast, some of the best times of my life and my artistic career, and I certainly wouldn't have been able to do it alone. I very much appreciated, and appreciate, their own hard work and talents in bringing so many really cool shows and short films to life. I also have to give a big thank you to Brett Hitchcock and Denny Hitchcock for taking a chance and letting us do late-night R-rated shows at the Speakeasy during that 2003-2007 stretch, when before that, it had only been used for the decidedly G-rated Comedy Sportz. And, of course, I'm very thankful for all the phenomenal actors, actresses and crew I worked with on all those productions. It was definitely a good time, and I couldn't have done it without you.

I also want to thank my collaborators with QuadCities.com — the awesome team of Steve Holmes, Trevor Bertucci, Tess Abney, Tristan Tapscott, Jonathan Turner and Khalil Hacker. You're all fantastic, and I love working with all of you!

The arts, especially the performing arts, are a collaborative field, and while projects can be driven by individual artistic vision, we're often helped along by those who struck the trail before us, and those alongside us on the way. It does not diminish your own achievements to acknowledge that, it raises them within the context of a larger scene of creators. And, it's just the right and courteous thing to do.

So, I want to say kudos to Rein, for doing the right thing, however small, but nevertheless significant, in giving that credit.

Taylor Swift Offers More Than 'Folklore' About Her Illuminati Ties

July 31, 2020

Listen, I know what you're thinking.

You're thinking, "Wow! Taylor Swift just released a new album! I wonder which ex-boyfriends all her songs are about?"

Oh, you naïve child.

Taylor Swift's songs have never been about ex-boyfriends, any more than Planet Ping Pong's pizza menu has been about pizza.

Of course, those of us who aren't SHEEPLE all know Taylor (I can call her Taylor) has long been a tool of the Illuminati, and her songs have incorporated secret coded metaphors for the takeover of the world.

"Blank Space?"

About people having their memories erased and reprogrammed by 5G.

"We Are Never Getting Back Together?"

About the breakup of NATO and the downfall of society necessitating a New World Order.

"Shake It Off?"

About battling the CORONAVIRUS.

"I Knew You Were Trouble????"

Well, ok, that one's about Harry Styles.

The art for Bjork's new record, cleverly disguised as a Taylor Swift album.

But aside from the odd song about her exes – Harry Styles, John Mayer, Jake Gyllenhaal, Erik Estrada, Herve Villachaise, Taco, Chickenzilla, Animal from the Muppets, Mother Theresa, the Dalai Lama, Harry Potter (if he existed), Larry Dallas, Greedy Gretchen, Caillou, etc. – most of her songs are part of an elaborate global conspiracy to brainwash the population and prepare them for world control by the reptilian shape-shifting elite.

The MK Ultra-controlled singer is constantly dropping truth bombs in her music and public persona, not the least of which is that her most popular album is called RED (red being a known Illuminati color; don't believe her lies that it's just a tribute to her devotion to Big Red cinnamon gum).

But as Q, through QAnon, begins peeling back the veil on the horrible secrets of the world, it seems Swift may be changing sides, perhaps breaking out of her mind control box and truly becoming free, joining such resistance artists like MGMT, Beastie Boys, Tenacious D, and Yo Gabba Gabba.

In fact, Q might have a follower in Swift (who took her pen name from Jonathan Swift, another famous creator who tried to tell us about the clandestine hollow earth and its denizens who emerge periodically to influence human civilization).

You can see the evidence of her shift right there in her new album, folklore, which dropped last week.

132

Sometimes you just gotta be happy for finding a nice secluded place to go fart.

Looking at the song titles you see a definite pattern emerging, in which Swift is actually revealing who the mysterious Q has been all along.

No, not Vanilla Ice.

But good guess.

No, no, not David Hasselhoff, but, ok, good guess I suppose.

NO, NOT WILLIAM HUNG!

DAMN IT, LET ME FINISH!

Are you ready?

Have you settled down?

You get your juice box and your goldfish open? Ok. Ok.

The person who the mysterious Q has been all along is . . .

A lot of people are sharing this on their social media as evidence JFK Jr. is back after faking his death. I can see why, because that's such a rare hand gesture.

John F. Kennedy, Jr.

That's right.

JFK Jr. began getting involved in politics in the 1990s, and as rumors and momentum began to build about him potentially running for office, he realized in 1999 that he was a target of the same deep state that assassinated his father. So, Junior faked his death, and went into hiding.

He was helped along the way by a secret underground of anti-deep staters who have been wanting to free the American people from the control of the Illuminati for decades.

But now, now, he's finally about to come forward, as the voice of Q, and the man behind the plot to take back the world.

And Swift is acting as the John The Baptist to his Jesus with her new album.

Just look at those song titles:

The Last American Dynasty: Obviously a reference to the Kennedys.

Exile: Talking about how JFK Jr. has been in exile all these years but is ready to return.

My Tears Ricochet: Talking about how sad he was about his father's assassination and how he's returned to get revenge.

Illicit Affairs: About Marilyn Monroe, another MK Ultra controlled celebrity who helped set up JFK for assassination.

Taylor Swift appreciates the softer side of JC Penney's new spring dresses.

Invisible String: About how Q, a.k.a. JFK Jr., has been a shadow puppet master all this time.

Hoax: All about how JFK Jr. faked his death and went into hiding, keeping up the hoax all these years.

Epiphany: Once revealed, the world will realize that JFK Jr./Q is here to save them.

Peace: A new era of world peace will be ushered in, as the deep state, the illuminati, and their minions (e.g. Nickelback) are defeated.

Mirrorball: Ummm, JFK Jr. used to go clubbing a lot. And once the world has been brought to peace and harmony again, we're all gonna party! Yeah!

So, there you have it. Totally obvious, blatantly apparent, evidence that Taylor Swift has broken her MK Ultra programming (you GO, girl!) and is now an agent of Q, helping QAnon save the world. And I've brought you the story and done my part to help.

You're welcome.

Now if you'll excuse me, now that I've dropped those truth bombs on you, I've got to get started on my next brilliant expose, uncovering the insidious clandestine messages in THIS SONG...

Especially During Covid,

Q-C's Small Businesses Need

Your Support

August 7, 2020

Things are not looking good for this fall in regard to covid-19. Numbers are spiking, the government has been pathetically inept in terms of dealing with the crisis, and the economy is once again on the verge of completely tanking. Unemployment is up, some industries are shut down through the end of the year, and others are teetering on the precipice of being shut down, maybe for good. I don't know about you, but I'm so pessimistic I'm starting to stock up on toilet paper.

That's why it's more important than ever to shop at your locally-owned small businesses now.

Local businesses aren't just the economic and entrepreneurial life blood of an area, they offer you a world of new adventures you're never going to find anywhere else. And if variety is the spice of life, the Quad-Cities offers you a pretty ample spice rack that's full of delicious flavors for you to enjoy.

Yeah, yeah, yeah, I know. I see your eyes rolling, "ANOTHER damn patronizing editorial about shopping local, blah blah blah…" and I know, I know, you don't want the lecture. I know, I'm not your Dad. The DNA tests came back negative. I remember.

But this isn't a patronizing editorial. Just the opposite. I'm telling you to shop local because you want the best. And you're going to get that by shopping local — especially since all of these shops are taking great pains to make sure your experience is safe, conscious and preventative of any covid risks.

When it comes to eclectic, funky local shops, stops like Fred and Ethel's, Major Art and Hobby, Mellow Blue Planet, and Tim's Corner are bursting with vibrance and character. There's really no comparison when it comes to locally-owned brew pubs and bars vs. your chain restaurant lounges and the like. If you're looking for a great drink, Icons Martini, Wake Brewing, RIBCO, Radicle Effect, Midwest Ale Works, Bent River, and a host of others are fantastic. Pretty much all the performing arts venues are closed up, but Circa '21 is offering periodic shows and virtual shows, and Rozz Tox and Kavanaugh's have small-scale stuff and both offer cool — if diametrically different — vibes.

And of course, for locally-owned media that covers the local scene and offers virtual performance spaces, virtual art galleries, a virtual writers studio and more, you can't beat your source for fun, FREE, local entertainment and features, QuadCities.com. (Like that little plug there?)

Listen, I get it, nobody shops completely local all the time, because quite frankly there are some non-locally owned items and services that you can't avoid, but the more you can, the better. Ok, maybe some hardcore people are giving me the condescending snake eye now, snooting their noses up and saying (i.e. lying) that they ALWAYS shop local. And well, if that's you, good for you. If you vape smoke signal me by the end of the week, your locally-hand-drawn certificate of pretentious hipness will be delivered by a locally-bred pigeon to your hobbit home to avoid the use of a printer or computer made outside of the Quad-Cities and a federal mail service based in Washington.

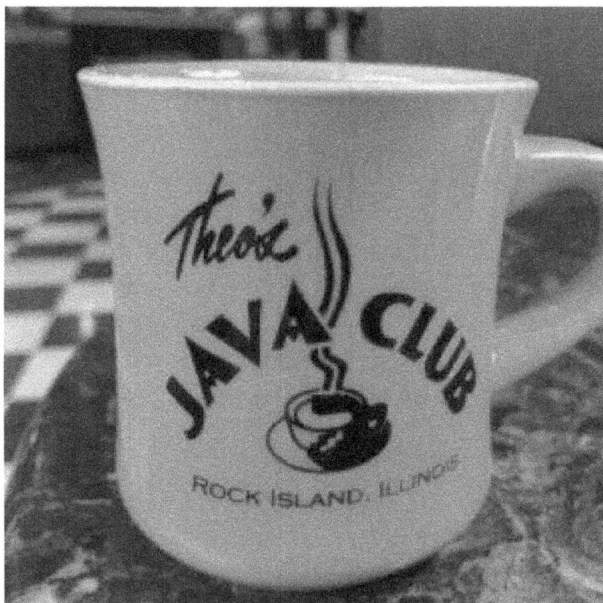

But as for the rest of us who live in a world that doesn't include the phrase artisanal toilet paper, we shop a combination of local and chain. When I want my groceries, I predominantly go to HyVee (local), but Aldi (big box) has got some fantastic stuff and some great bargains. I mean, really, if you don't Aldi, you're missing out. If they're having a big sale on produce, I'm going to go there to pick it up. (Hey, listen, you can't beat 49 cents for avocados.)

I love my Theo's and Cool Beanz, but sometimes I also get my daily caffeine fix from the Colorado-based Caribou Coffee. I mostly cook at home, and typically when I go out to dinner, I always go to a local restaurant like Curry Out, Big Swing, Le Mekong or La Rancherita. But I've also eaten lunch at Subway and late on a Saturday night after the bars have closed I have been known to hit the Taco Bell drive-thru. I love Olde Town Bakery, but if they're not open, I'll roll Dunkin Donuts. If I've got the choice between a big box and a local business, I'm going to shop local, especially since they're offering me something I can't get anywhere else. And especially since I, myself, have been a local businessman for almost two decades. But I recognize that there are some items that are easier to pick up at a big box, and sometimes, especially when you're in a rush, convenience rules.

And so it goes. It doesn't make you a terrible person. Those big box stores do contribute local taxes, and employ local people and their jobs are dependent upon our business. Well, okay, if you only shop big box and never shop local that does make you a person that should really get out and expand their world – trust me, you'll thank me later for the restaurant recommendations here, and really, any of the local Mexican restaurants are terrific – but in my experience, those people are as rare as their opposites.

I've been an entrepreneur and run local businesses for over 20 years now. I've run a local publishing company, ran a local magazine and two local websites, run two theater groups and comedy troupes and currently am a co-owner in the local online site you're reading. I also run a local tutoring company that offers free help to at-risk kids, a local theater company and a local publishing company. As the operators of Theo's, Cool Beanz, Blue Cat, Icons, HyVee, Olde Town Bakery, Tim's Corner, La Rancherita, Major Art and Hobby and dozens of other local businesses can tell you, I've been a loyal local shopper for my entire time in the Quads.

So yeah, I'm biased towards local businesses. But it's not just a political or ethical bias, it's because those businesses offer awesome things. They're not just great LOCAL businesses, they're great BUSINESSES. They don't need some sort of special treatment just because they're the local guys, they should be treated with the same respect and regard as those big boxes, and, actually more, because they are pure entrepreneurs who have started from nothing and built it from the ground up, and they're working their butts off to put out a quality product.

And they do. Nothing at Chili's is going to match the specials at Big Swing – and for the same price or less. (I recommend the meat loaf – damn great stuff.)

The reason Chi Chis and Carlos O'Kelly's went sombrero down is because people realized they could get much better and more authentic food from the myriad local Mexican restaurants around here. (I'm mostly a Nally's, Habaneros, El Patron and La Rancherita guy, but all of them are great.)

And while Applebee's can advertise their giant, watered-down fishbowl drinks all they want, Icons martini bar is going to kick their butt on taste and quality every time. (The traditional martinis rock and for something different, the pineapple chipotle is freaking amazing.)

And for a HUGE, awesome guide of local restaurants that offer carry-out, pickup and covid-friendly service, check out our list here on QuadCities.com. (Also, if you own a business that we don't have featured, please contact me at Sean@QuadCities.com so we can get you listed — FOR FREE!)

That's why you should shop local. Not because they're the little kid who strikes out every time that everyone cheers for because he makes the effort. But because they're hitting home runs and hustling out every hit. Because they're just as good if not better than the competition.

So do yourself a favor.

Shop local, especially now when they really need your help. It's how you find unique flavor and it's always an adventure to try those new things you're never going to find anywhere else.

Your new favorites await you . . .

The Answer To One Of Life's Deep Questions Is Under Your Nose

August 14, 2020

Ever walk into your house after you've been away, or walk into a room and notice a strange smell?

That happened this week, after the Midwest hurricane knocked three trees and multiple branches onto my house and around my yard. The power was out, my phone was out, and internet was (and still is) out, and my son and I walked around outside later that evening, after the storm had cleared, to check out the damage in our own yard and around the neighborhood.

When we arrived back in the house, before dark, there was a strange smell.

145

"Was that you?"

"No, was it you?"

Nope on either.

Now, of course, once you do encounter a strange smell in your house, you have to try to find it, because who wants a strange smell in their house?

I'll usually look for some dropped food or something behind or under furniture, and sometimes that's the case. Some bit of stray potable that tried to escape and sadly discovered its motion was limited to whatever got it there in the first place, and then was left, saddened and chastened, to rot in bitterness and disappointment. It's like the Willy Loman of pizza toppings. Poor green pepper. You coulda been a contender.

But what if it's not a rogue vegetable?

My next guess is that it's a croaked mouse. They'll get into the house from time to time, especially in the winter, and will end up kickin' it, and not in the sense that they put on Hammer pants and break dance. And once they get to a certain ripeness, they'll emit a foul stench.

But what if it's not a mouse?

Something else? Something in the vent? Something downstairs coming up through the vent?

Nope, nope and nope.

Whiff your underarms.

Not you.

Not me.

Did you fart?

No.

You sure about that?

Then what is it?

Maybe it's a ghost?

Do ghosts fart?

I've often wondered about this, since ghosts seem to engage in some fairly banal and goofy activity. People will talk about ghosts leaving cabinets open or opening kitchen drawers or moving little items around.

Because of course that's not the people in the house, who have just forgotten they left a kitchen cabinet open.

It's ghosts, dammit!

That always seems strange to me. If ghosts do exist, and our energy forces transcend our physical beings, and if our ghosts can travel anywhere across the world or the universe, and have the expanded power of our energy unencumbered by physical bodies or concerns, wouldn't you think there would be more exciting things to do than open people's cabinets and knock crap off the walls?

I don't know, maybe those ghosts don't have much imagination. Many people don't, so maybe that limited focus continues on into the afterlife?

So if some ghosts love spending their time doing goofy, little stuff like that, playing practical jokes and such, why wouldn't they step into a room and pop one?

Why not get someone to blame the other person in the room for their farts? Or get them to think there's something else going on, and then ghost giggling as they look around and under the furniture? I mean, really, if you're a ghost, you must get bored. Playing practical jokes on people is probably one of the highlights of your day. Otherwise why bother opening and closing the cabinets?

So my vote is that yes, yes, ghosts probably do fart.

And aren't you glad that incredibly important question has been answered?

Oh, and the smell?

Food gone wild in the powerless fridge.

Much scarier.

I Could've Been The Kid In The Bullying Video

August 21, 2020

Bullying.

I revisit this subject, and this column topic, every year around this time, because every year, a new school session starts and invariably the potential for children abusing other children rises. Even this year, and maybe especially this year, due to covid-19 and the inherent pressures and stresses surrounding it, the potential for kids to lash out and hurt others is heightened.

A couple years back, The Keaton bullying video went viral. It brought tears to my eyes and broke my heart.

As anyone who went to junior high with me knows, I was bullied mercilessly seventh and eighth grade years. I was a skinny, awkward, artsy, goofy kid with messy hair who loved art, writing, comic books, science-fiction, manga, soccer, Dr. Who, David Bowie, Duran Duran and all kinds of other so-called "geek things." I was poor and had ripped clothes and went to a rich kids' school. I was pitifully awkward with girls and terribly insecure about my looks. Oddly enough, I was a good athlete but it didn't help much. I was still too weird to be accepted by anyone but my own clique of nerds and geeks who were also hunted and tormented.

I had little to no support at home or school. The typical response from both was "stop being a wuss" or "that's what kids do, deal with it" or "it'll build your character."

It didn't build my character. I thought my character was just fine.

It made me learn to hate people and hate myself. It made me angry and depressed. Which is a pretty sad state to be in when you're only a 12-year-old kid.

Two people helped me. My writing and art teachers. They taught me that my strangeness and my talents were good things and that it was ok to be an outsider. I looked at famous people like David Bowie and Prince and they helped inspire me. They were unique and unapologetic and so I would be the same. To hell with other people. I was going to be me.

Dr. Who, George Carlin, Andy Kaufman and John Lydon inspired me with their humor and the way they reveled in their outsider status in gleeful and fun fashion, and so would I. I was tired of apologizing and trying to fit in because I just couldn't.

150

I was a horrible failure at being anything but me.

Fortunately, that's what I'm best at.

And that's how I've been ever since.

Ironically, the same "geeky crap" that got me tormented ended up being some of the same things that found me my tribes later on in life. The people that really loved me and connected with me.

By senior year of college I was first runner up for homecoming king at a college of 27,000. Me. The skinny little unpopular freak who was called ugly and stupid not that long before.

And I didn't get there by changing to fit in with other people.

I got there by being myself and not caring about the opinions of others.

So to anyone out there being bullied: Don't compromise. You're not the one who needs to change. THEY ARE. To hell with them. You're beautiful because you're unique and they're jealous because they're afraid to be, or, even worse, deep down they're scared that they're not.

To anyone out there who can make a difference in a kid's life: Do it. Be that person! Be that mentor they need, that I had, that helped save me.

And to creative people: Don't compromise your vision, be honest and embrace your unique character. Because it's that honesty and bravery and courage that inspires others and helps us feel less alone.

Having been the bullied, I make sure that now that I'm in the position to be a mentor and a creator, I follow my own advice.

Bullying is not to be accepted nor condoned. It's a mental and emotional disorder that needs to be eliminated. The false mythology that it's part of some rite of passage or tied in with some obscene, ridiculous concept of masculinity is perverse and ignorant and needs to be dismissed entirely. There's no reason for bullying.

There seems to be a common misperception that being against bullying is to be against any opposition or to coddle children and adults. It isn't. The important thing is to teach children, and adults, how to disagree and accept and face challenges in a productive manner. CONSTRUCTIVE criticism is good. Challenge is good. Competition is good. Debate is good. That's how we evolve and grow our ideas and within the arena of academia it's imperative that all ideas and opinions be sharpened and challenged to reach the pinnacle of veracity. Likewise, facing against intellectual, emotional and physical challenges can provide us with the impetus to grow. But there are productive ways in which to do that, and it's imperative of parents and our educational system and society to teach people the most civil and productive ways to do that.

Bullying offers neither a civil nor productive way to aid evolution. As numerous studies show, it merely creates imbalances in personas and leads to further dysfunction.

It needs to be eliminated. And steps need to be taken to facilitate that elimination immediately. It shouldn't take a viral video or a column like this to point that out. It should be common sense and based upon the decades of evidence taken into account.

Everyone deserves to live their life and pursue their happiness. As long as you're not hurting yourself or anyone else, be happy. Life's too damn short to be anything else.

Let people find their joy. Let people have their joy. Let people be happy and live their lives.

● ● ● ● ● ● ● ● ● ● ● ● ● ● ● ●slghvl0

Is Katy Perry Hiding A Really Big Secret?

August 28, 2020

Katy Perry didn't just kiss a girl and liked it, she faked her own death apparently and liked that too.

And why the hell not? Everyone needs a hobby.

As we thankfully roll into the last quarter of this craptastic year, the conspiracy theories just keep getting weirder and weirder. Some of them are pretty harmless and dumb, like people questioning whether Netflix conspired with China to create the Coronavirus (It was that bitch Carole Baskin, idiots! Geez!), and others are more along the dangerous and irresponsible side, like, ya know, certain print publications running cover stories telling people they shouldn't wear masks in the middle of a pandemic.

There are definitely some that are gaining far more traction than others, like Q-Anon. I told you a few weeks back

154

about Q-Anon positing that Tom Hanks, Oprah and Ellen, among others, are pedophiles, and that Wilson the volleyball is actually code for some satanic ritual.

Another biggie that keeps getting put out there on the interwebs and social media is that Q is none other than John F. Kennedy Jr., who allegedly faked his death in a plane crash, befriended Donald Trump, and, along with him, plotted to wait more than three decades to finally take down the Deep State that secretly assassinated his father. Why did he wait this long? I guess he had to catch up on watching all those episodes of "Friends" he missed.

Anyway, climbing the charts again on TikTok in recent weeks, in between girls dancing to a song saying they want to be f**ked to sleep, is an oldie but goodie about pop singer and "American Idol" judge Katy Perry.

No, it's not the logical one, that she and Zooey Deschanel are twins separated at birth. (I've talked to my longtime secret girlfriend Zooey about this, and we've both had a laugh several times over it. She's quirky and impish, don't ya know!)

Satan Demands A Monte Carlo is my new band name.

And no, it's not the kind of routine famous person one, that Perry gave up Christian singing because she sold her soul to the devil to become a huge megastar, and he told her to sing about lesbianism, just to make Jerry Falwell Jr. mad, because Falwell was hoping she was going to have a breakout hit about banging a cabana boy while her cuck husband watched. (At this point, even the devil is bored with that one; currently he requires not just your soul, but your left pinky toe, three of your best memories, a 1986 Chevy Monte Carlo, and your ability to taste cilantro.)

No, no, no, the conspiracy theory that's been making the rounds on TikTok and elsewhere lately is one that started back in 2014, when a YouTube video presented "compelling evidence" that Katy Perry was actually none other than child beauty pageant winner JonBenét Ramsey, who according to "fake news" reports, was murdered in her home on Christmas of 1996.

One of the many YouTube videos talking about the puzzling conspiracy theory that Katy Perry is JonBenet Ramsey.

However, according to the "real news" of the conspiracy theorists, JonBenet was not murdered, and in fact she, along with her parents, faked her death as part of an Illuminati cover-up, and the Illuminati turned her into a mind-controlled drone through Project Monarch, who then became the pop star Katy Perry, since all pop stars are mind-controlled drones used to push the Illuminati way, satanic changes to society, pumpkin spice lattes, Gap clothes, and the slang word "jerkin'!"

Now, this may seem to some of you like the plotline to the movie "Josie and the Pussycats," (which is really underrated, seriously), but no, these people actually think that Katy Perry is secretly JonBenet Ramsey.

Evidence includes the fact that they're both entertainers, they look somewhat alike (I guess? Maybe? It's hard to say since JonBenet was 6…), Perry mentioned JonBenet briefly in her biography (joking about how she was a performer at a young age similar to JonBenet), and they have the same eyebrows.

Yeah.

Same eyebrows.

"In the latest episode of 'Twin Peaks'…"

Not kidding.

Another reason given is that <u>Katy Perry has repeatedly said she does not like pineapple on her pizza, and</u> JonBenet Ramsey, according to investigators, apparently <u>was possibly killed over a pineapple.</u>

Yeah.

Now, a lot of women have the same eyebrows, because those brow places at the mall do a hell of a job in regard to consistency. I mean, really, my brows have never looked more delicate and sexy, honestly, hats off to you, Shecky's House Of Brows And Nails, bra-vo!

And, let's completely ignore that Katy Perry was born Katheryn Elizabeth Hudson in October 1984. Let's also ignore that she was a Christian pop singer who released her first Christian pop album *Katy Hudson* in 2001, and she had a few more subsequent releases and record contracts that went nowhere until her breakout. After all, the

Illuminati work in mysterious ways, and they have rapid aging technology that could've just taken little "JonBenet" and put her into a hermetically sealed container of dove's blood, Oil of Olay, and Kayo, and turned her into Luke Skywalker, I mean, a teenaged Katy Perry.

We can also ignore the fact that JonBenet's parents and Katy Perry's parents are still alive and not the same people, because the Illuminati can create mind-controlled clones (DUH!)

We can also ignore the band Blind Melon, because their original singer died and they haven't had a hit in decades.

But what we REALLY can't ignore is the incontrovertible evidence that Katy Perry and JonBenet Ramsey CANNOT be the same person.

JonBenet thinks the dress is white and gold, and Katy thinks it's blue and black.

It's white and gold. Jesus, people!

Should You Judge Someone

On Their Musical Tastes?

Sept. 4, 2020

There's a scene in Nick Hornby's "High Fidelity" where the lead character, played by John Cusack, asks whether or not it's fair to judge people largely on their music tastes.

So, is it?

What kind of music do you like?

Who are your favorite singers?

What's your favorite song?

When I was younger, particularly in high school and early college, I was inclined to judge potential friends and girlfriends in large part on their musical and pop-culture tastes.

Yes, I was an entertainment snob. Hard to believe, I know.

In comparing preferences in music, TV shows, movies, and books, I felt you could tell a lot about how much you would have in common in other areas. Each of my favorites reveals a defining trait about me. An idealism. An ideal. A passion. A way of looking at the world. A way I work, a way my mind and heart moves.

To some extent, this is still true. As I think it is for most people. Look at someone's list of favorite books, TV shows or music, and you learn a lot about that person.

Certainly, this may seem superficial, but then again, so is basing attraction solely on each other's physical attributes, and that definitely hasn't gone out of favor.

But what if there's something more to this? What if a person's inner workings, chemistry and physiological proclivities actually are revealed by these things?

Stick with me here.

We, as human beings, are in our essence a series of molecules that are mostly empty space. If you look at an atom, it's a tiny nucleus surrounded by protons and electrons that are once again, quite small. In between those solid bodies? Nothingness.

So, what holds us together?

Movement. Vibration.

Our atoms vibrate at a set rate that makes us solid. This is science. It's proven. And likewise, it's also been proven that certain vibratory states or exposure to certain sonic sensations elicit certain physical reactions. It could be something as simple as a pounding bass driving us to the dance floor or something as complex as the military firing microwave pulses toward an oncoming army to cause headaches.

So, if this reaction to vibration unites us, if our bodies are so entwined with these vibrations, wouldn't it make sense that those of us who react strongly to certain vibrations — i.e., musical styles — would share a certain body chemistry or rate of vibration that produces a similar reaction?

And likewise, couldn't that be transferred to literature, which is a series of words, symbols for sounds that likewise create similar vibrations either internally or externally?

And if we share a certain vibratory state, wouldn't it make sense that we might share other similar physiological and psychological traits?

Ergo, we would have more in common.

So, maybe it's not so far-fetched to think that if you and another person have very similar musical or literary tastes, you may have more in common with that person on a deeper level.

Just something to think about the next time you're on a date and someone asks you what kind of music or books you like.

Even if you like Nickelback.

Downtown Rock Island Is

Ripe For A Renaissance

Sept. 11, 2020

Denny and Brett Hitchcock are the most tenacious of entrepreneurs.

For over 40 years, their business, Circa '21 Dinner Playhouse, has endured a handful of recessions, booming and barren economic conditions, and, now, a pandemic.

It certainly hasn't been easy. Especially not in 2020.

Both father and son have said, without hyperbole, that their business was very much in danger of going under if pandemic and economic conditions continued.

164

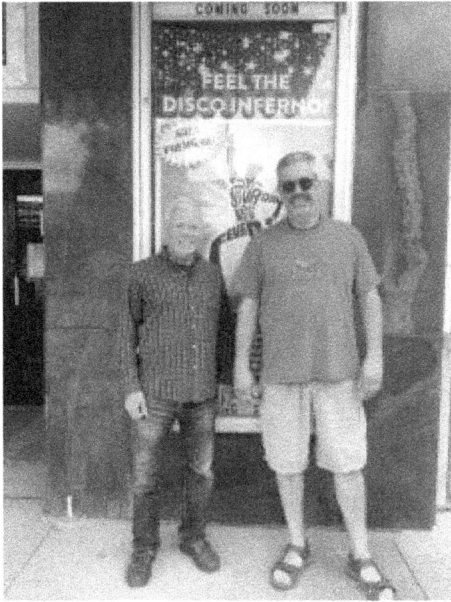

Denny and Brett Hitchcock at Circa '21, 1828 3rd Ave., Rock Island.

However, this week, they re-opened, after several months of stress and uncertainty. They debuted a new show, "Savannah Sipping Society," a homey comedy that's got the heart and humor to make it a success in times that are sorely lacking in both. (You can pick up tickets for the show, running through Nov.7, at www.circa21.com, and by calling (309) 786-7733, ext. 2). Their smaller spot next to Circa, the Speakeasy, has begun to debut small shows, and both, with some navigation and social distancing, are hopeful to see great crowds. Already, Circa's numbers are showing promise.

"People are hungering to get back to the theater again, to get things back to normal, or as close to it as we can get right now," Brett said in a recent interview.

And so, once again, the Hitchcocks – who it should be noted aren't trust fund kids, aren't running a not-for-profit, and are very much invested in their business as their sole income – have made it through a crisis with determination and grit, and in doing so, have kept an anchor of downtown Rock Island alive and thriving, offering several dozen employees homegrown jobs keeping the Quad-Cities economic life going.

And their story could very well be the story of downtown Rock Island.

Once thriving, now struggling, but with tons of promise, and the opportunity to be a jewel of the area bringing in hundreds of local jobs.

I thought about this as I was walking around the downtown the other day, while I was waiting for food at Healthy Harvest Urban Farms, the best vegetarian café in the area, and one of the best restaurants as well. Located at 1616 2nd Ave., it's just the kind of unsung treasure that Rock Island has long needed, and one which fits the downtown's style as an eclectic, creative, bohemian landscape.

As I was walking around the downtown, noticing all the funky, cool architecture, and all the empty buildings, I couldn't help but be reminded of a trip I took a couple summers ago to Boulder, Colorado.

Boulder, like Rock Island, once had a downtrodden downtown. But now, it's amazing. Over several blocks, you can pop in to a variety of awesome retail shops, restaurants, coffeehouses, cafes, and, yes, dispensaries. It's got a diverse crowd, a chill vibe, and it's open and thriving day and night.

A full crowd attends the Aug. 16 Music on the Marquee at Circa '21.

It's everything downtown Rock Island could be.

At one point, the District was THE place to be. In the '90s, when I first moved out here from Chicago, it was one of the reasons I bought a house in Rock Island, because it was where I constantly hung out. Spots like RIBCO, Blue Cat (now Big Swing), Copia (now Icons), Huckleberry's, Circa, The Speakeasy, Theo's, Steve's, and more, were habitual haunts for me and my friends. Over the years, Rozz Tox has been added to the list, along with Wake, just outside the downtown area, and a world-class, beautiful outdoor area has been created along the riverfront in Schwiebert Park.

A lot of those spots are still there, still vibrant, still doing great things. But there are too many empty spots between them. However, those spots offer opportunities, for even more terrific places for people to go.

There's plenty of downtown housing, plenty of downtown space, and plenty of potential. Rock Island has got a smart, forward-thinking mayor in Mike Thoms, an alderman for the downtown with energy and vision in Dylan Parker, a strong relationship with the downtown business association, and more. It just needs people who are going to walk down its sidewalks and see the potential I did, and do. And I have faith that before long, those people are going to emerge, and that's going to happen. It's just going to take some tenacity, vision, and action.

And when it does, there will be Circa '21, and Denny and Brett Hitchcock. The visionaries, the entrepreneurs, who have seen it all, struggled through all the tough times, and emerged with their dream still alive. Never forgotten, always an anchor, a building block, upon which will once again rise a vibrant arts and entertainment district, and a jewel of the Quad-Cities.

Netflix' 'Social Dilemma'

A Dark Mirror Of Our World

Sept. 18, 2020

There are very few shows you can deem "must see" anymore, although not as much due to their quality, as due to the fact that not many shows can truly be described as being targeted for a wide audience anymore.

We live in a world that's become increasingly fragmented and subdivided, and invariably there are few things upon which the vast majority of the population can agree. Entertainment used to be the great uniter of the people. When television began to rise to prominence in the '50s and '60s, cultural touchstones were based upon events it showcased.

The Beatles on Ed Sullivan.

The finale of "M*A*S*H."

169

Who shot J.R.?

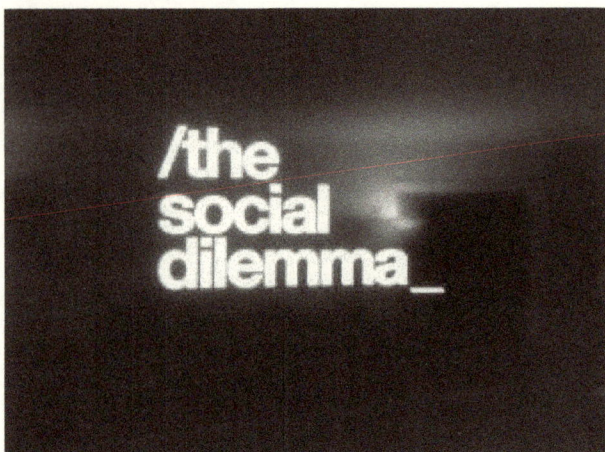

Even going beyond the pop cultural sphere, people of a certain age can remember uniting to watch the Berlin Wall come down, OJ Simpson's Bronco chase, and the constant coverage of 9/11.

Part of the ubiquity of those experiences was due to the paucity of selections available. At one point, strange as it may seem to anyone born beyond the year 2000, there were only three major television networks, and even for my own generation, Gen X, we grew up with four if you add in PBS, and a couple of extras like WGN and two or three UHF channels if you grew up around Chicago or New York as I did. Even when Fox debuted in the late '80s, it was seen as a novelty, much like the CW and UPN a decade later. So you didn't have much choice in the matter, and that led to greater commonality in regard to taste, opinion, and community of experience.

For better or worse, that world has been flipped on its head with the advent of cable TV, and then, the Internet, which brought a vast array of choices into people's lives. But with

170

those choices came greater divisions, as there were few touchstones upon which we could all land, and all agree upon. The ratings numbers for the top television programs and radio stations have been steadily diving for years as people, given a plethora of choices, have become more divided than ever in their individual preferences.

This seems a trivial thing, and you may wonder why I'm starting off this column this way. But think about it: There was once a time when our differences in politics, religion, and other hot-button topics could be overcome by talking about the pop cultural touchstones we had in

The rising number of teen suicides, depression, and other mental health issues is addressed in 'Social Dilemma.'

common. A trek to the in-laws' could be navigated by talking about sports. Kids and adults could find common ground in watching "Family Ties" every Thursday night. Family get-togethers on holidays could find common ground in chatting about movies or shows that most everyone had seen.

Now, we're more divided than ever. Get-togethers are dominated by people sitting around disappearing into their own worlds on their cell phones. And even when those phones are temporarily banned for the ostensible sake of conversation, the times are strained, as common topics of conversation seem harder to grasp.

The practice of not only widening these gaps, but manipulating and monetizing them is the subject of the most provocative and hard-hitting film of the year, one which I wholeheartedly encourage everyone to see. The movie is called "The Social Dilemma," and it's currently available on Netflix.

"Social" begins by rolling out its cast of real-life characters – a veritable who's who of behind-the-scenes power brokers in social media and internet sites over the past two decades. Every platform from Facebook to Twitter to Google and more is represented by multiple employees, all of whom describe in detail how those platforms began, or at least how they began with those platforms, with altruistic intentions of literally uniting the world, only to see the opposite rapidly take place as the algorithms of those sites were used to divide and subdivide groups and create pods of opinion reinforcement to cultivate viewers as attention chattel sold to advertisers.

They go into how facts are largely ignored in the interest of keeping people hooked and locked into dopamine surges created by rousing their emotions, and stoking conflicts to increase screen time, allowing them to sell more advertising and addict their customers.

The result has been an online society divided along stark lines to increase the delineation of demographics for ad sales. In addition, it's also

172

Tristan Harris is one of the social media experts interviewed extensively in the documentary.

stoked insecurity, fear, and the sense of lacking within people, which only makes them more suggestible and ripe to be sold things which are marketed as the answer to their needs. The more desperate and wanting someone is, the more they seek something to assuage that. That in essence is the life's blood of advertising new products and it's become all the more starkly achievable given the sophistication of the artificial intelligence systems running popular websites, allowing them to quickly build a personality profile of users and prey upon their weaknesses.

The film shows how the sites very intentionally and concertedly do that, and also how they can be weaponized to manipulate public opinion and even help overthrow governments and cause social unrest. It also shows how that culture of incompleteness and need being created has caused record depression and suicide among young people who are most tied into the networks.

In all, it's a chilling, fascinating, and thought-provoking film, and one that truly fits the description of must-see, given the ubiquity of the internet and social media in our lives, and our desperate need to understand its true motives and how to disengage and put it into perspective to reclaim our own ability to think and live independently.

Although certainly ominous, the documentary ends on a hopeful note. Each of the people involved, all of whom has been intimately entwined with the technology inherent to the medium, talks about how it can be a force for good, and what changes can be made to tip the scales back in that direction.

Will that happen?

It's hard to tell.

But the first step to solving a problem is to identify it, and "The Social Dilemma" is a vital and important first step in doing that. I highly, highly recommend that anyone involved with social media in particular watch it, and consider the message it has to offer.

Ready For The Untold Story

Of Einstein's Sister?

Sept. 20, 2020

Throughout this week, we've been featuring stories on Quad-Cities band Einstein's Sister, which is releasing its first record in almost two decades this weekend, during Record Store Day at CoOp Records in Moline.

The band – Kerry Tucker, Bill Douglas, Marty Reyhons, Steven Volk, and Andy Brock – is releasing a double-A side single, "Standing Still" and "Begin Again," on transparent blue vinyl.

But that's one of the only ways in which the band has been completely transparent.

Throughout this week, I've been scanning the archives and corners of the internet for information on this "Einstein's

Sister," in an effort to present to you a complete picture of this band that many of you, especially those of you who haven't reached puberty yet – which may or may not include some members of the band – haven't discovered yet.

But now, well, you're about to discover more than you bargained for.

You're about to get all you can eat of Einstein's Sister.

Ok, wait, that didn't sound right.

You're about to get a full buffet of Einstein's Sister.

Hmmm, not quite there yet.

The last thing Bea Arthur ever saw.

You're about to find out THE SHOCKING TRUTHS AND SECRETS BEHIND THE BAND EINSTEIN'S SISTER!

Now THAT'S better.

Especially the caps and exclamation point. Now that looks like something a real internet weirdo would type. Thank you for the suggestion, Perez Hilton. And for telling me I had spinach in my teeth. Maybe not so much thank you for putting your hand in my mouth to try to take it out. But, the thought was there.

Anyway, here are THE SHOCKING TRUTHS AND SECRETS BEHIND THE BAND EINSTEIN'S SISTER!!!!!

- Producers have to utilize a special microphone and effects on the vocals of their records because lead singer Bill Douglas insists on performing only with a full beard of domesticated honeybees gently caressing his chin and vocal chords.
- Guitarist Kerry Tucker served a short stint in prison when he met the "cash me ousside" girl ousside and repeatedly berated her, demanding to know what Dr. Phil smelled like. During his time in prison, he often asked to be placed in solitary confinement, where he could be found with a sanguine smile on his face, his lips with the barest hint of a whisper, a sole word upon the wind of his breath: "Elderberries."
- Bassist Andy Brock has often claimed to be St. Louis Cardinals great Lou Brock, going so far as to don an old-timey uniform, carry around bags of peanuts and yell "Let's play two!" at inappropriate moments. Much to the chagrin of his wife.

- The group was originally called Einstein's Fuckhead Little Brother and Einstein's Racist Alcoholic Uncle before settling on its current moniker. Another name considered was Studmaster Trolley and the Circle 8's. Yet another name considered was Meth.

-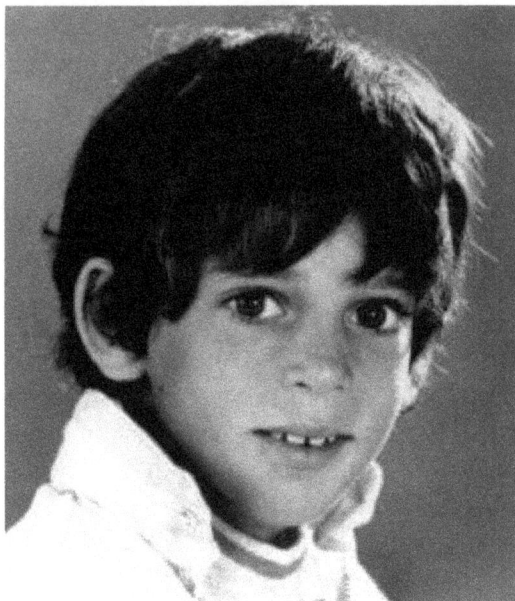

THE Jeremy Gelbwaks.

Drummer Marty Reyhons is obsessed with equaling the drumming skills of the legendary Jeremy Gelbwaks. In fact, so much so that after every take on their first album, he would pester his bandmates, repeatedly asking, "Goddamn it! Was it as good as Jeremy Gelbwaks???" The band and producer Tom Tatman became so incensed with his strange perfectionism and obsession with Gelbwaks, which included him nicknaming each of his drum kit parts Jeremy, and often wearing a t-shirt emblazoned with the insignia "Not As Good As Jeremy Motherfuckin' Gelbwaks," which he bought at the hot press lettering t-shirt shop at the mall, that Tatman and the band plotted his murder. However, they quickly decided against it, due to the fact that they didn't have a reasonable place to hide the body, they figured his Mom might come looking for him, and, well, Marty's just a swell guy. So they came up with an alternative plan, which they use to this day. After every take, one of the band members comes up to Marty, puts a hand on his shoulder, looks him in the eye, and says, with sincerity and solemn gravity, "Marty, Jeremy Gelbwaks would be proud." Then they give him a Werther's butterscotch candy from the sweater pocket of Bill's cardigan, and somewhere, an angel gets its wings.

- If you play their vinyl album of "Learning Curves" backwards, it sounds terrible. No, really, don't do it.
- All but one of the band members is allergic to Whoopi Goldberg.
- Kerry Tucker leads an active social life outside the band, so much so that he's often asked to consult on the settings of female hygiene product commercials. Tucker enjoys careers as a racing jockey, an in-demand club DJ, and a mother of two who recently served jail time for embezzling close to $2 million. He also enjoys parkour, a fine pear brandy, and the music and lyrics of JoJo Siwa.
- Andy Brock is sometimes so ornery, he once shot a man for snoring too loud, he often bites down extra hard on gummy bears because

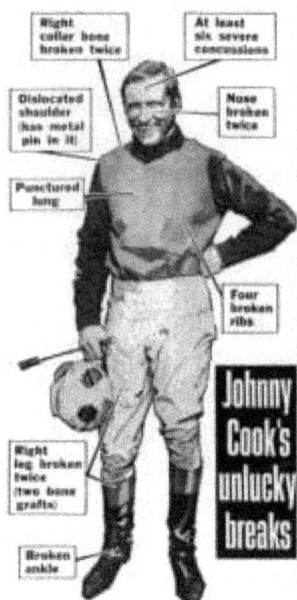

Inside the illustration:
- Right collar bone broken twice
- At least six severe concussions
- Dislocated shoulder (has metal pin in it)
- Nose broken twice
- Punctured lung
- Four broken ribs
- Right leg broken twice (two bone grafts)
- Broken ankle

Johnny Cook's unlucky breaks

Kerry Tucker posed for this.

he once read a story on Huffington Post that they actually feel pain, and he'll sometimes tell children that Santa Claus doesn't like them. But, he'll do it in Mandarin Chinese, so they can't understand it, because he's really not that bad of a guy once you get to know him.

- Their album "Humble Creatures" was a concept record about Caillou tripping acid and discovering we actually live in a virtual simulation created and manipulated by Paw Patrol.

-

This asshole again.

Guitarist Steven Volk wasn't included on the current record, in large part because he's been dedicating his time to his passions of origami, horticulture, and creating life-sized sculptures of Wilfred Brimley out of Quaker Oats. Several of his sculptures are on display in New York's Museum of Modern Art and in the collections of such renowned cultural mavens as Iman, Yoko Ono, and Carrot Top.

- Bill Douglas is also known for his artistic talents. He has a website called DrawMeBill, which features several portraits of celebrities, including Taylor Swift, Jennifer Lopez, and Jennifer Lawrence. An odd trait of his portraiture is that all of the pictures are done from at least 50 feet away from the subject.

- The band has actually had several of its songs on MTV, played in the background of a number of the station's reality shows. In fact, in the group's official bio, Douglas and Tucker say that one of the highlights of their career, that actually brought a collective tear to each of their eyes, was when they heard a beautiful and sensitive love ballad they'd written played during a scene of "Jersey Shore" where Snooki found out that The Situation had given her crabs.
- Each one of the band members has a tattoo of a different member of Limp Bizkit somewhere on his body. And when they put the tattoos together, it imbues them with a very special power – the ability to get in for half price at the Chorus Line Strip Club, as well as unlimited trips to the Early Bird breakfast buffet.
- All of the guys have an excellent sense of humor, and are great sports for allowing me to joke with them in this way. I wholeheartedly recommend you head over to CoOp Records in Moline on Saturday and pick up a copy of the excellent double-A side single, "Standing Still" and "Begin Again."

Tell Marty that Jeremy Gelbwaks sent ya.

QC Time/ Lo//e/ Do Not

Bode Well for Economy

Oct. 2, 2020

"If you work in the media, you're going to get fired."

My college Journalism 101 teacher said that to our eager group of 18-year-olds on my first day in his class.

Great way to introduce us to his curriculum, and the business, right?

He told us it wasn't meant to be a cautionary statement, merely a pragmatic one.

That's the business.

That's media.

Ownership changes, management changes, budgets get cut, formats and directions get shifted, and the people in the trenches are the ones who are usually set loose.

You have to have a thick skin, a backup plan, and the ability not to take it too personally, because usually it isn't. Usually it's just business.

Unfortunately, lately, business has not been good.

Especially for daily newspapers and radio stations nationwide over the past decade and particularly during the time of covid.

And certainly not for those in the Quad-Cities this year.

As I wrote about in January, when Jim Fisher, and several others, were fired, radio in the area has basically lost the ability to call itself a "local" media, slicing its staffing down to the bare minimum and replacing it with syndicated programming.

But it's not just radio.

It's all media, which has been impacted by an increasingly corporate environment driven by a national rather than local focus, that prioritizes overall company profits over the needs of the individual communities in which it has outlets.

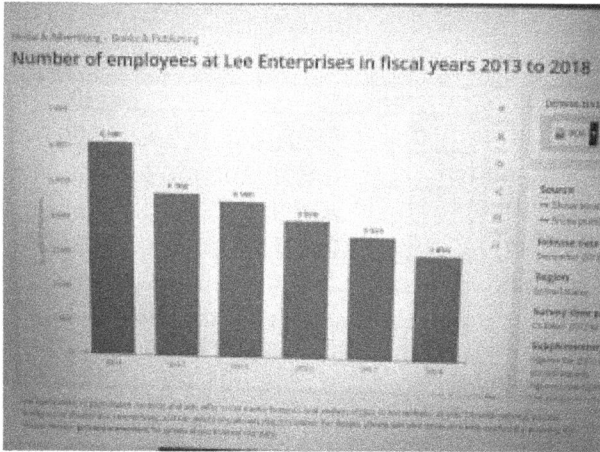

Number of employees at Lee Enterprises in fiscal years 2013 to 2018

Lee Enterprises, which owns the local Times and Dispatch/Argus, went from 6100 to 3056 employees between 2013 and 2018.

At this point, I've worked in the media since I was 11 years old, when I began writing for newspapers and magazines nationwide. I went on to work for more than a dozen radio and television stations, first around my native Chicago and Los Angeles, and then here in the Quad-Cities and beyond.

And yeah, I've been fired. Or, rather, let go, laid off, downsized, or whatever euphemism they've used for getting canned.

It's part and parcel of working in this business.

And it's one that's become all-too-common this year if you're working for, or perhaps not working for as the case may be, Lee Enterprises.

The owner of the local Quad City Times and the Newspaper Formerly Known As The Dispatch And Rock Island Argus (but which is now basically the exact same

185

paper as the Times only with a different masthead) is now the fourth largest owner of newspapers in the United States, according to the Lee Wikipedia page. Lee has an august and storied history, founded 130 years ago, in 1890, by Alfred Wilson Lee, and along with formerly-Small Newspaper Group-owned The Dispatch and Rock Island Argus, were not that long ago part of a vibrant and bustling local newspaper market. During the halcyon days of the 1990s and into the mid-late 2000s, the market was served by the dailies the Times, the Argus, and the Dispatch, as well as major weeklies the Leader, Bettendorf News, and the North Scott Press. And that's not mentioning the television stations, or the fact that during that same era there were far more locally-produced radio programs on the airwaves. The result was a robust cornucopia of communication in the market and a well-informed and in-tune population. If something happened in the area, you undoubtedly knew about it, because at least one, more than likely several, of those outlets were covering it.

The Rock Island Argus building was once a bustling hive of activity and home to a thriving media outlet. In 2008, it closed its doors.

However, those days seem very long ago, as most of those publications are gone, and Lee has fired more than half of their employees over the past seven years. The amount, scope, and depth of news coverage and information available in this area has severely declined.

According to Statistica.com, the number of employees at Lee Enterprises papers shrunk from 6100 in 2013 to 3056 in 2018. That's a 50 percent cut in employees in just five years. According to Bloomberg.com, the latest statistics show the number of employees at Lee to be 2786, which is another nine percent slash in two years, and a total 55 percent plummet in staffing since just 2013.

That number of people employed is likely going to be even lower once it gets updated at the close of 2020, because this year, and particularly this month, has not been kind for many good folks at the Times, who have been fired and "retired," many after several decades of service.

I certainly know how they feel. In 2008, the Rock Island Argus building closed down, moving all its employees to the Moline Dispatch office. Between 2008 and 2009 they let go roughly 100 people, and I was one of them. A decade later, in spring of 2018, after seven years with Lee Enterprises' newspapers the Quad City Times, Bettendorf News, and Muscatine Journal, I was cut again, along with about a dozen other people at the time.

Since then, it's been a sad ritual at the end of each financial quarter. About every three months, more layoffs. More cutbacks.

Earlier this year, Jonathan Turner was let go, and we are very fortunate to have had him join us on our team at QuadCities.com. He was one of many in the spring. Then there were a few more in the early summer. And now, more in the fall. This past September has featured some of the biggest losses for the Times. My very good friend Linda Cook left after 35 years at the Times to pursue another opportunity. John Marx also left to pursue another job, likewise after 35 years. Several other long-time employees like Jennifer DeWitt and Laura Anderson Shaw

We at QuadCities.com are fortunate to have Jonathan Turner on our team after he was cut loose by the Times earlier this year.

were fired or retired.

The unkindest cut was perhaps Lucinda Resnick.

Resnick had announced her retirement a few weeks ago, planning to bid farewell on Jan. 1. She only had a few months left. Instead, she was fired in late September. After 48 years of service.

Imagine that. Imagine pouring almost half a century of your life into a job. Putting that much time, that much energy, that much of your existence into a business.

Forty-eight years.

Then you get to the end.

You've earned your retirement.

You make plans and announce you're going to leave.

And you're not even allowed, after almost five decades, to go out on your own terms. You're kicked out a couple months shy to save the company a few thousand dollars in salary.

But, as my journalism professor once said, that's the media. And it's something that's been accelerated at an incredible rate over the last decade for a variety of reasons, and pushed to an even more disturbing level this year during the covid pandemic as the real economy — as opposed to the artificially-inflated numbers of the stock market — has crashed.

However, it's not just the media.

Not anymore.

It's the entire communications industry, and the vast majority of entertainment, arts and leisure organizations, which are struggling and dying after being blasted by covid.

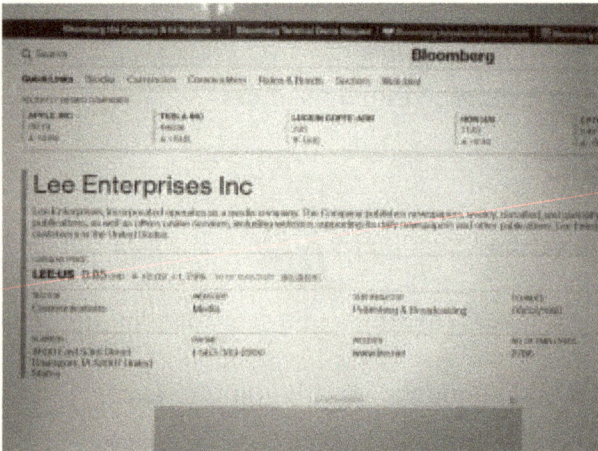

Lee Enterprises has gone from 3056 employees in 2018 to 2786 in 2020, according to Bloomberg.

It's small businesses nationwide, many of which have had to close permanently due to the pandemic. It's Disney laying off 28,000 employees. It's local teams like the River Bandits, Steamwheelers, and Storm having to cancel their seasons. It's the TaxSlayer and other venues canceling their shows and events. It's dance clubs and bars like Billy Bob's shutting down for good. It's places like Circa '21 and The Rust Belt and others barely hanging on.

It's gig workers, and teachers, and actors, and performing artists of all types. Struggling. Trying to get by. Not knowing what's going to happen next.

These aren't freeloaders. These aren't people who don't want to work. These are people whose jobs are gone. Gone. Some permanently. And some, even more excruciatingly, are in limbo, leaving the workers left wondering if they have anything to wait for, holding on, wondering if they should move on or wait.

This has been an especially brutal year in that regard.

Which is why it's all the more important for the government to take it seriously.

Politicians from both parties need to step up for the people they've been elected to represent.

These aren't people looking for "free stuff," as so many ignorant and cruel commentators have accused from their perches of privilege.

These are people who have paid taxes, who have had their money taken by the government ostensibly to provide these types of services when they need them. That's what tax money is for. That's why we're taxed. To provide funding for such services so that they're there if we ever need them.

And at this point, a lot of people are very much in need of them.

People in the media. People in the arts. People in all walks of life. All of them important. All of them vital in their own way.

We haven't been immune. We at QuadCities.com have certainly been hit hard by the pandemic, as all media companies have. Fortunately, we've been able to stay afloat, and have continued to provide quality features and coverage of the area arts and entertainment scene, but it hasn't been a smooth ride, and we've had to take actions bracing for the road ahead. And at this point that's crucial. Not only for our business, but to ensure a better informed and educated public.

It's crucial to have an active and thriving local media. The public needs to be informed on what's going on, whether it's governmental news, updates on the pandemic, or any other of a variety of important topics.

It's likewise crucial to have the arts and entertainment scene — and, as we at QuadCities.com strive to provide, active and thriving coverage of that scene to support it. What would you do without local concerts, local theater, local sporting events, events for the family, outdoor events, not to mention movies, TV, books, music, digital shows, live music, performing arts and media? How would you relate to the world, find out about the world, be a part of the world beyond that right in front of you? How would you find escape when that world is far from ideal?

And at this point it's pretty far from ideal.

Unemployment numbers are at record highs. One in ten people are unemployed. An average of 850,000 per week filed for unemployment in September. In JUST THE LAST 24 HOURS, over 70,000 people have been laid off, including workers from Disney, American Airlines, United Airlines, and more.

Many people have been let go. Many are taking unpaid furloughs. Many are left waiting, on hold, until the pandemic finally passes, and with numbers of the infected and dying beginning to rise in many states and overseas, and scientists predicting a second wave of covid in the fall and winter as temperatures drop and more people are stuck inside, there's a sinking feeling that we're seeing the history of earlier this year repeat itself.

If it does, if there are more shutdowns, if things slide backwards to where they were in the spring, what's going to happen? How many more local businesses are going to be hit? How many more jobs are going to be lost in the media? In the entertainment industry? In general?

It's not going to be good.

"If you work in the media, you're going to get fired."

If you work in any field, at this point, the same thing could be said.

And the more it's said, the more it happens, the more dangerous it is for our economy, our collective outlook as a society, and our world.

And the more it's said in the media, the fewer people will be around to inform us about just how ominous it's becoming, and to give us hope about how we can get through.

● ● ● ● ● ● ● ● ● ● ● ● ● ● ● ● ●ſlghvl0

Netflix Haſ Nailed The

Covid Zeitgeiſt

Oct. 9, 2020

Are Netflix executives reading our minds?

There's been an eerie pattern throughout the pandemic, in regard to the most popular programming emerging on the streaming platform. In an uncanny way, it's mirrored the attitudes and zeitgeist of society at that time, especially over the past year during the time of covid.

Certainly, some of it can be chalked up to unconscious needs and preferences being manifested in viewing choices — of people being attracted to certain programs at certain times and them becoming popular because the vast majority of us are feeling a certain thing at different times, and those programs fulfill a need for us, whether through escape or catharsis.

194

But it's also been strange to watch, as programs have emerged and been added on Netflix that just so happen to perfectly nail that which we need and want to watch during these bizarre and uncertain times.

It's been said there are no coincidences.

All actions, all events, are part of a lattice of connection that perhaps we can't see, and of which we're not aware, but that we all feel, consciously or unconsciously.

That's what it means when you say something feels right. It feels like it should be. It feels like it should be of our time.

That seems to be true especially when it comes to entertainment. To be sure, at all times, there is popular entertainment. There is always something moving through the transom of our lives, of our consciousness, taking up the spotlight. But there are so few of those avatars of popular culture which become truly transcendent, that go beyond mere popularity to become not just ubiquitous but somehow perfectly fitting for that particular time. The Beatles. Disco. Nirvana. Reality TV. TikTok.

It's why the four most resonant programs during the covid-19 pandemic have been "Tiger King," "The Last Dance," "Cobra Kai," and "The Social Dilemma."

On the surface, they couldn't be more disparate.

"Tiger King" was garish and lurid, the tale of seedy and strange zookeepers, rivals who no one could really root for, but who captivated our attention with their sensationalistic and selfish battles while behind-the-scenes, the alleged reason for their being, the tigers, were abused and used as props for their power plays. Sound familiar? It should.

"The Last Dance," on the other hand, was bittersweet, beautiful and nostalgic, the story of one of the greatest athletes in the history of sports, and the way his farewell was tainted, ending an era in a sad and regretful way that still feels like an open scar.

"Cobra Kai" was bathed in nostalgia as well, a yearning for simpler times, but it went far beyond that to cast that nostalgia in a revelatory and unfamiliar light, showing that the good old days weren't as good as we thought, and in addition to that, it also demonstrated that people are complex beings that evolve and change.

Finally, "The Social Dilemma" was by far the most serious of all of the shows, forcing us to look into the black mirror of our screens and the way social media has insidiously poisoned our society in so many ways.

All of the shows have mesmerized viewers like no others during the past two months.

And when you look at the last seven months, it's not difficult to see why.

196

The time of covid has been chaotic and difficult, unprecedented in all of our lifetimes. It's left people completely confused and feeling a strange sense of unease, because we have no reference point to it. None of us were alive and cogent during the last true pandemic over 100 years ago, and even if we were, the times have changed so much it would almost be irrelevant as to how each has impacted society.

Wars, recessions, political attacks, social violence, environmental disasters, those, sadly, have been mapped for us, and, also, sadly, we've become almost used to them, we take them in stride. However, this is new territory. We've never seen this particular virus because it's something new, we've also never had a pandemic shut down governments and economies so thoroughly or have something we couldn't truly control or get a handle on have such an impact on society. We also haven't had anything like this happen during a time when people were all online and the spread of disinformation and the feeling of not knowing who or what to believe was so pervasive. It's left people feeling very uncertain and adrift.

And so, whether consciously or subconsciously, we seek some stability to bear this time out.

Most of us had no choice but to weather it inside, and most of us turned to our televisions for escape and subconscious catharsis.

And that's why these shows have been so popular, because they've been so relevant to that catharsis.

"Tiger King" came at the beginning of the pandemic, when everything was chaotic and unknown. We had no idea how to deal with this new normal. It was bizarre and unwieldy and, for many, frightening. We had no bearing to navigate it.

'Tiger King's' Joe Exotic: A man for our times.

And in the midst of the frenzy emerged this show, which was completely chaotic and bizarre and unwieldy and, underneath its oddity, perverse and frightening, dealing with killing and violence and bloodshed.

But through watching it, we could escape. Not just in terms of entertainment and vicarious thrills, but through using it as a conduit for all the uncertainty and chaos of that early part of the quarantine.

Through all the chaos of "Tiger King," there was humor, there was levity, there was some sense of being able to step outside the turbulence and stand watch as it happened to someone else, and in being able to do so, it made us feel better about ourselves and our worlds. Subconsciously, perhaps, it was a way of laughing through fear and uncertainty. But there was also something that struck a familiar chord for us. In many ways, we were the tigers, the ostensible reason for being for this world, watching as our leaders from various sides squabbled, fought, grasped for power, and trafficked in the ridiculous and audacious, all while we were left to just wait and see how this circus was going to affect our well-being. We had little to no control over it, so at best all we could do was laugh at the absurdity and chaos of everything. "Tiger King" gave us an outlet for that.

Eventually, however, things somewhat stabilized. We began to embrace the new normal. It became easier for us to get by, to navigate the strangeness of the new world, with all of the social distancing and masks and working from home and everything else that went along with it.

But along with acceptance and assimilation came an air of sadness.

Came a recognition of loss.

Once we were able to navigate our new world, once we were able to get beyond the initial shock – the fight or flight mechanism that honed our attention to only that which was pertinent to the here and now – we were able to think, to feel, about what was happening.

And that wasn't necessarily a good feeling.

'The Last Dance' scored big audiences for its poignant tale.

We thought about the missed graduations, and birthdays, and sports seasons, and our friends and family, and just our normal lives and being able to do things we'd always taken for granted.

We were surviving, we were navigating it, yes, but it wasn't our ideal. It wasn't what we wanted.

And that's where "The Last Dance" came in.

When was the last time things were truly good for us and our country?

The '90s.

Before 9/11. Before the endless wars. Before the umpteen recessions and economic collapses. Before the bloodthirsty divisiveness and hatred between sides. The virulent tribalism of the internet. The superficiality and insecurity fomented by social media and reality TV. The constant "scandals" pushed to goose media ratings. The huge economic divides.

The '90s were, for most of us, the last time things seemed good, or even seemed like they had the hope of being good, beyond any cynicism.

The Chicago Bulls of the '90s and Michael Jordan represented that idyll. They were the prominent sports and pop culture heroes of our time. Watching that show reminds us of where we were then, and who we were then, both as individuals, and as a nation.

The economy was great. We weren't at war. We certainly weren't in quarantine. The cost of living, the cost of college, the cost of everything, was far lower. And while there were definitely political and social divisions, as there have been for centuries, they weren't anywhere as vicious as now, and they weren't being flamed by the ubiquity of opinions on social media. It was a pre-9/11 world. And it was a pre-ubiquitous internet world, where the new technology we were just learning about was full of nothing but hope for a better future, a better time, a better life for all of us.

Watching "The Last Dance" isn't just about watching the Chicago Bulls. It's about taking a time machine back to a time when things were so much easier and simpler. The last time we could actually, truly, say that.

And, like "The Last Dance," like the end of those Chicago Bulls and Jordan's career, it feels like it ended far too soon, and was taken away from us long before our time, by forces beyond our control.

And we miss it. We miss having that hope, that opportunity, that world that seemed so much easier to navigate.

And in watching Michael Jordan, one of the greatest athletes in the history of any sport, a man who worked relentlessly, with incredible loyalty, to build not just himself but his organization, from nothing, many of us feel some sense of community with him. We think of the years of our lives spent poured into hard work, unpaid overtime, incredible loyalty, to companies and businesses and a way of life, only to see it rewarded with job loss, a lack of appreciation, and a venomous condescending arrogance. When Jordan spits out Jerry Krause's line about "organizations winning championships" being used to dismantle one of the greatest teams ever, he's not just speaking for the Bulls, he's speaking for all of us who have seen offices full of great, hard-working people at the tops of their games get capriciously and cruelly cut away.

It's been a sight all-too-familiar during this pandemic.

And it's caused people to evolve in ways they never saw possible, re-evaluate what they once thought of as the path to the American dream, and look at their lives and how they and others have changed and had to evolve.

That's when "Cobra Kai" came around, in late summer and early fall, as this "new normal" was making us question if there was ever really any normal at all, or if it was all an illusion.

'Cobra Kai' emerged as one of the best-written and thoughtful shows of the year.

That's one of the biggest subtexts of "Cobra Kai," which looks at the black-and-white, heroes-and-villains world of the "Karate Kid" movies in a far different, new, and complex light. It doesn't just show where the characters are now, it follows them as they reveal themselves to be all-too-human and full of both glories and flaws. It also re-examines the entire past of the series from different perspectives to show that not everything was as clear as we thought. As we look at the past through the perspective of once-certain-villain Johnny Lawrence, we see that once-certain-hero Daniel LaRusso wasn't as perfect as he was painted, and Johnny and his fellow Cobra Kai weren't completely bad but were more products of their backgrounds.

This came as more and more people were forced to look upon their own lives, and their own choices. Imagine being that person in their 40s or 50s or beyond who was laid off their job. I've certainly been there. You did everything right. You followed the American dream. You worked hard, you did everything you were asked, you put in extra overtime, you did everything society and capitalism demanded of you and instead of getting the success and security you were promised by the system, you were betrayed and cut loose, fired and screwed over, just as you were nearing your retirement, the capstone of

The faceoff between Johnny and Daniel was given new context in retrospect that fit into the ambiguous times we live in.

all the time you spent doing "the right thing." It made you re-examine those priorities and whether or not what you were fed was just a bunch of crapola. "Cobra Kai" does the same thing in re-examining its own past mythology.

And, much like people have had to adapt and evolve, so do the characters in "Cobra Kai," and they do so in ways that are messy and not always easy. They try and fail. They attempt to do the right things and they don't work out. They question their actions, and wonder whether it's worth it to bother. Just like so many of us have done during this time.

Most recently, as we've neared the fall, and election season, and the threat of a renewed pandemic and covid suffering, there emerged the darkest documentary to capture our attention among all the shows listed here. "The Social Dilemma."

Most disturbing because it's based in thoroughly-researched fact, it shows us a very dark picture of how we've become such a divided society and has given a very clear explanation as to why, going into this election season, going into the dark pit of a second wave of the pandemic, people have been so ready to discard facts, science, reason and rationality in lieu of conspiracy theories, pseudoscience, and nefarious

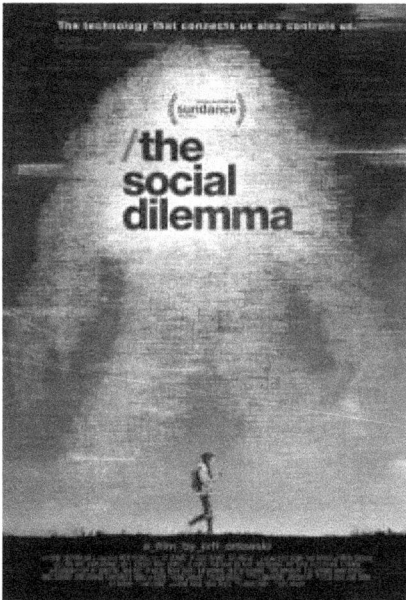

The poster for Netflix's "The Social Dilemma."

schemes of manipulation. It's not the most pleasant picture, but it's one we need to face when asking ourselves how we got here, because facing it is the only way we can take action and change things for the better.

"The Social Dilemma" is not pleasant, but neither are the undercurrents of our society right now. Just yesterday, the FBI uncovered a plot to kidnap and kill the governor of

Michigan. More than two dozen high-ranking politicians, including Donald Trump, have contacted covid. There's still no sign of an economic relief package even as millions of people continue to lose their jobs and statistics show that up to half of the small businesses that existed in our country on Jan. 1 of this year could be out of business for good by Jan. 1 of the next. These are dark times, that need to be addressed to be rectified, and the only way to do so is through addressing them factually and accurately in order to change them. "The Social Dilemma" presents that same bitter pill. And it's poignant that during this time that message has resonated to the point where the documentary was the top-rated program among all streaming programming over the past month.

Just like "Tiger King" was during its time.

Just like "The Last Dance" was during its time.

Just like "Cobra Kai" was during its time.

It's always difficult during times like these. It's often impossible for many of us to express our feelings, to put them into words, or even fully

'The Social Dilemma' is disturbing and provocative.

express that we even feel them. But they're there. And oftentimes, whether consciously or not, we seek out entertainment, alleged escapism, in the form of some catharsis, that allows us to watch and experience these things and to get those feelings out through the characters on screen, through the things going on in these movies and shows.

When nobody knew what to expect, when everything was a surprise, when we desperately wanted to be able to laugh in the face of fear and the potential of something horrible, "Tiger King" was there, giving us constant surprises that we could laugh at and that entertained us, and an underlying tone of terror that we could experience with distance and a dark humor, like the catharsis of a horror film.

And as we came to grips with that, as we began to really mourn and feel the bittersweet nature of life during covid, there was "The Last Dance," to allow us to feel those same things through the people in the film, somehow wishing they could go back, for one last dance with that era, and yet knowing they could only look back and wonder, and hope that someday, things would be right again.

Then as the year progressed and job losses became untenable and disillusioning, there was "Cobra Kai," to make us re-examine our pasts and how they related to our present, and to try to navigate our way through uncertain times and come to terms with not just our own imperfections but those of the world around us.

Most recently, as we near an even darker time, there was "The Social Dilemma," to shine a very bright and often uncomfortable light on our society, to bring us to terms with it, so that hopefully, we could change it.

Each has reflected us at the time we were watching it. And in some ways, each one reflects the way we are now. Wondering. Uncertain. Hoping that someday, things will be right again. Trying to find answers, solace, some sort of structure in a very nebulous and shifting world.

That's the role entertainment plays for us.

That's how it touches our souls, our hearts.

That's why it's important to us.

And that's why it's been so important to us during this time. Because we've needed it now, more than ever. And we still do.

● ● ● ● ● ● ● ● ● ● ● ● ● ● ● ● ● slghvl0

Enough With The Political Crap, Pass The Stimulus

Oct. 20, 2020

I'm sick of the politics.

I'm sick of the politicians.

With more people struggling than ever, with more businesses closing, with the covid numbers increasing yet again, just like the scientists predicted (amazing how you can listen to intelligent, learned people and get accurate predictions on what's likely to happen, isn't it?), IT'S TIME TO PASS ANOTHER STIMULUS BILL TO HELP PEOPLE STRUGGLING FROM COVID.

A familiar sign around the Quad-Cities and across America this year. Politicians fiddle while the Rome of small businesses burn.

I wrote another story today, one of probably over 100 this year, about a business closing down due to covid. This time it was Big Swing, in downtown Rock Island, not exactly a bustling hub for business activity due to a variety of reasons, covid's impact being one of them. Big Swing is right down the street from Billy Bob's, which just closed down not that long ago.

As I've written before, I'm sick and tired of writing stories like this. I'm sick and tired of seeing people I care about, businesses I enjoy, local entrepreneurs I admire, suffer needlessly due to this pandemic. And yes, it is needless. These places should be getting help. These people and places pay taxes. Those taxes go to the government. When they're suffering, that tax money they've been paying all these years should go BACK to them to help them out. This isn't a handout people are asking for. This is a return on the money they've been paying into the system for years. And it's a good financial move by the government, because it's small business and the folks working for those businesses that keep local economies going, that keep the working class vibrant, that keep those tax dollars coming in because of the number of businesses and employees rising.

And Big Swing, Billy Bobs, places that have just closed, are potentially just the latest. I'm friends with a lot of business owners. They're hurting. They're cutting hours. They're cutting costs. A lot of them are just hanging on. And I don't want to keep writing these stories about people I care about, about businesses that help keep our community socially vibrant and financially stable.

Once a thriving club packed with people on the weekends, Billy Bob's closed recently due to the massive impact of covid.

When those businesses and jobs are eliminated, more people have less money in their pockets for bills, for rent, for mortgages, for disposable income to support other local businesses. With the businesses eliminated there goes more sales tax eliminated from the city coffers. There goes more income tax eliminated from the state and federal coffers. And if you live in Rock Island, Rock Island County, there goes an even bigger budget deficit that could result in your property taxes going up, which could result in more people either leaving or not wanting to come to Rock Island, which continues the string I just put out there.

It always stuns me when people cannot see the basics of situations such as this. But then again, most people aren't taught these things in school, and many people are too busy believing ridiculous conspiracy theories about Tom Hanks being a pedophile satan worshipper to actually learn about civics and the things that have a measurable impact upon their lives.

Such as the true nature and job of being a politician.

You look at the Washington politicians in their ivory towers, receiving government-paid healthcare and government-paid salaries, and the first thing to realize is that "government-paid" means paid for by YOU. It means that YOU, the taxes that you pay, whether in income taxes, sales taxes, property taxes, whatever, are the one footing the bill for government spending.

Ergo, YOU are the one paying these politicians.

YOU pay their salaries.

YOU pay for their benefits.

They are YOUR representatives, YOUR employees.

They are called public servants for a reason. They are elected to serve YOU.

Not to stand over you, not to stand apart from you, not to use their office to become millionaires by receiving legal bribes from big businesses to give those businesses your money in corporate welfare, but to serve YOU, represent YOU and your needs. It is not reasonable nor rational to send millions of people to Washington to vote on items of interest. That's why politicians exist, because the system was created for people to vote on who they wanted to go to Washington to represent the interests of those people giving them their proxy, to fight for and stand for what they need.

So what are your needs right now?

Looking at recent polls, SEVENTY PERCENT of you are in favor of more stimulus spending to help the people and businesses in need due to the negative impact of covid upon them.

But there hasn't been a stimulus bill since the spring. Instead, we've gotten the customary dicking around. The Democrats passed a bill for $3.4 trillion in the spring. Trump seemed to concur that stimulus was needed, and many Republican economists were likewise in line with the need for another stimulus package. However, Mitch McConnell and the Senate Republicans, since the pandemic at the time didn't impact their rich puppet masters, sat on it and did nothing. Then the Democrats passed ANOTHER bill, for $2.2 trillion, in response to McConnell and the Senate Republicans complaining that the first bill was too expensive, because when it comes to actually helping people, they're suddenly fiscally tight. As opposed to when it comes to blowing up people in needless wars overseas, in which case, there's a bottomless pit of money to spend. That was also dismissed by McConnell, even as he and his wife took taxpayer dollars they didn't need from the first stimulus passed.

Secretary of the Treasury Steven Mnuchin has been among those consistent in support of a second stimulus bill.

Then as polls turned against the Republicans, they came back to the table. To his credit, Secretary of the Treasury Steven Mnuchin has seemed to be one of the few Washington folks to actually understand how desperately a second stimulus is needed. He and Speaker of the House Nancy Pelosi have begun negotiating again on another package, with one currently on the table for $1.8 trillion. Trump has gone back and forth on a bigger stimulus package, but seems to realize that his political future is tied to the economy and recognizes that he needs to get something done if he wants to stand a chance of winning a second term. Now, full disclosure, I belong to no political party. I'm a staunch independent and truth be told I don't think there should be any political parties because they encourage tribalism and ignorance and discourage freedom of thought and objective critical thinking. I've both agreed

214

and disagreed with Pelosi and Trump, I've tended to agree most of the time with Mnuchin, who has been the most rational and logically thinking of the group in regard to the pragmatism of the situation in my opinion.

But the fact of the matter is, we have a situation where 70 percent of the American public want their elected representatives to do something, and they are not doing it. And those who are holding it up need to be held responsible for their inaction, and how their inaction is negatively impacting their constituents and their employment, and their businesses.

Now, think about this for a minute.

Say you own a business. You are one of ten owners of the business. You make rules for the business by vote. Seven of the ten owners vote that the employees need to show up at 9 a.m.

Now say you're working in that business. And you don't show up at 9 a.m. Repeatedly. What's going to happen?

You're going to get fired.

The same way they should get fired.

Their 9 a.m. is getting a stimulus deal done.

Job performance review and potential dismissal is Nov. 3.

Get to work.

● ● ● ● ● ● ● ● ● ● ● ● ● ● ● ● ●/lghvl0

Is This Man Really A Time Traveler From 2485?

Oct. 23, 2020

There's been a long history of people claiming to be time travelers.

And there's been an even longer history of people just being full of crap.

Oddly enough, the Venn diagram between the two is almost an identical shadow of two circles.

Certainly, there are maybe one or two instances that have made me, and others, go "hmmmm."

But most of them have made me, and others, go, "Oh geez, this is friggin' baloney."

Art Bell: King of Late Night Media, Archduke of Lunatic Bullshit.

One of the most infamous of these among the bologna category was John Titor.

Now, back in the '90s and up to the mid-2000s, one of the most famous radio shows in the country (back when people actually listened to the radio in large numbers) was the Coast To Coast AM Show, hosted by Art Bell.

I absolutely loved this show. I used to work late nights at the newspaper back in the '90s and '00s, and I listened to Art's astonishing and often hilarious program every night. Art was everything you would want in a host of a show of this nature, he was sort of an odd and interesting character himself, and would expertly walk the line between cynical and incredulous when he interviewed a vast array of guests, everyone from people claiming to be alien abductees to people claiming to have caught werewolves to the occasional time traveler.

In fact, Bell was so into the whole time travel idea that he would, from time to time (pun intended) open up a phone line specifically for time travelers.

During many Bell shows, he dove into the stories of a mysterious character claiming his name was John Titor, which was actually a name thought to be short for "John TimeTraveler" that was used on several bulletin boards during 2000 and 2001 by a poster claiming to be an American military time traveler from 2036.

Titor made several incredible claims, including that he was here to help save the world from the Y2K bug, and that he was here to warn us

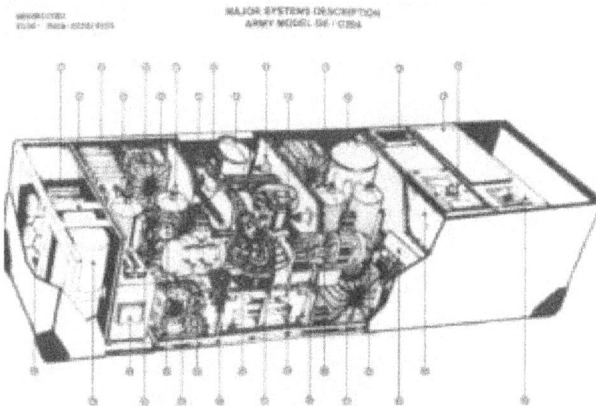

John Titor's alleged time travel device. Also makes toast and can chop onions like a charm!

about several calamities, including a nuclear war, mass famines, and the thriving career of Justin Bieber.

Of course, none of them came true, and it was later surmised that Titor was a hoax perpetrated by a couple of lawyers from Florida who were just goofing around.

I bring up Titor, because there's another time traveler who's been gaining a lot of attention lately in the world of TikTok, where there are several people claiming to be from the future, coming back to warn us about various awful things on the horizon, as if 2020 wasn't bad enough already.

This guy goes by the handle thatonetimetraveler, and claims to be from the year 2485, coming back to warn us of various events about to happen over the next few years.

In all likelihood, this guy is either yanking people's chains or doing a masterful job of jerking them along so that he can promote a movie, book, video game or something else tied in to the whole time travel thing and the world he's spinning for them.

And, fair enough for him. I don't really care, he's not harming anyone, other than anyone stupid enough to really take him seriously, and at the very least he's entertaining.

That said, let's take a look at a few of the things he says are going to happen over the next four years, which he's revealing to us as Imagine Dragons plays in the background, which is both hilarious and appropriate:

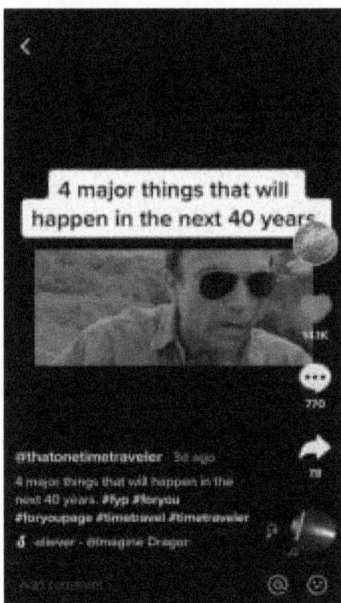

Majority of the cars will be electric, and It will also be illegal to drive gas powered vehicles.

@thatonetimetraveler · 3d ago
4 major things that will happen in the next 40 years. #fyp #foryou #foryoupage #timetravel #timetraveler
♫ gnrs · Believer · @Imagin

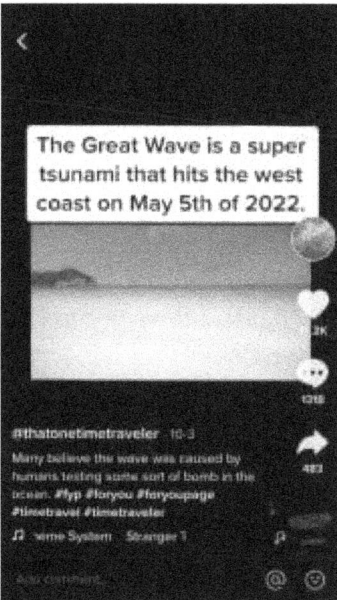

The Great Wave is a super tsunami that hits the west coast on May 5th of 2022.

@thatonetimetraveler · 10-3
Many believe the wave was caused by humans testing some sort of bomb in the ocean. #fyp #foryou #foryoupage #timetravel #timetraveler
♫ reme System · Stranger T

So, what do you think? Complete and total crapola? Partial crapola? Interesting or imaginative crapola?

I guess we'll find out. And soon. The guy says Trump is going to win the November election (although let's face it, he's got a 50/50 shot on that one; it's like picking the Super Bowl winner once you know the two teams that are playing) and he says some MAJOR thing is going to happen on Jan. 2, 2021. My guess is that it's the release of his book or movie or video game or whatever that he's promoting with this. Of course, if Trump loses everyone will think he's totally bogus, unless he comes up with some explanation of an alternate timeline or something.

I'll look forward to seeing that video, and as a time traveler myself, albeit one who only travels to the future one second at a time, I'm going to predict that the music he has playing during his explanation video is going to be this...

Quit Shaming All The

People Who Need Help

Nov. 13, 2020

One person is a man in his seventies, a true entrepreneur who took a massive risk and put in over four decades of long hours to build a business that became a hub of a local downtown.

Another person is a middle-aged woman who has been working since she was 16, and, over three decades, has put in countless hours working to build up her own business. And still another person is a younger man, who has also been an entrepreneur, starting up various businesses, who is one of the hardest working people I know.

All of these people exemplify what we like to call the American dream. They're the people that politicians hold up as positive examples when voicing their platitudes.

223

They're solidly working class, the backbone of our community and our country, and they stand as the pinnacle of the values we say we prize as a society. You work hard, you do the "right things," you persevere, and you will ultimately succeed.

Right?

Not always.

It's kind of difficult to do that at times, especially when you're hit by so many things out of your control. Such as a pandemic, and the uncertainty of state and federal officials trying to do the right thing in regard to containing it, leading to you having to close your business, or to you losing your job through no fault of your own.

And it's in this spirit that it's disgusting to me when I see people on social media and online criticizing these people with a broad brush. Posting ignorant comments mistakenly saying that getting stimulus benefits and the sort from the government is getting "free" stuff.

It's not. There's nothing "free" about it. It's getting back an investment on your money the government has been taking in taxes all the time you've been working.

Let me explain.

Now, remember when you were 15, 16, and first started working, and got your first paycheck? Remember when you looked over and were like "Who's FICA and why are they taking so much of my money???" That's the government taxing you. They've been taking that money for as long as you've been working. The government taxes you to pay for programs that are in the public good and your individual interest so that if and when you need them, they are there for you.

Some of the taxes go towards practical things like plowing the snow in the winter, or fixing roads and bridges, or providing police and fire service. A LOT of the money goes towards the federal military budget. Some of the money goes towards social programs, which are there as a safety net for people if they have unforeseen circumstances which put them in a place of needing them.

Such as now. Millions of hard-working people are out of work because their places of business, or their own small businesses, have been shut down temporarily or permanently due to covid and its ancillary negative effects on the economy.

These people have been working for decades in some cases, having that money, which has added up to thousands of dollars the longer they've been working, taken out of their paychecks. Those people who are needing to get unemployment and other benefits due to those circumstances are not getting free stuff, any more than you're getting free money when you withdraw it from your checking account. They're getting a return on an ongoing investment in the government system which has been set up as a social insurance for moments like these.

Are there people who abuse the system? Hell yeah there are. Just like there are mega-rich corporations and people who abuse the tax code and hide money in offshore accounts and get millions in government money each year despite making billions in profit.

But the myth of widespread fraud in the system is just that — a myth. Numerous studies have shown that the vast majority of the people receiving help from the government while under times of crisis are not on the programs for long, are eligible for them, and only utilize them when truly needed.

Much like the people who are suffering due to covid destroying the economy. Thousands of people locally and millions nationally have been put out of work. People in the entertainment industry, the airline industry, the restaurant industry. Basically any business involving interacting with the public in numbers larger than a couple dozen has been devastated. That's an awful lot of folks who have been fired through no fault of their own.

And to shame those working class people who have worked hard and are in difficult circumstances through no action of their own is wrong. To shame them for having to get help from the government is wrong. To shame them for having to be on unemployment or any other program is wrong. Have some compassion for them. Because "they" could easily be "you" someday. And given how covid has impacted everyone over the past year, that someday could arrive at any time.

Caribou Was More Than

Just A Coffee Shop

Nov. 20, 2020

We're all maps of our experiences, our lives a tapestry of our time spent. Every second, every moment of them.

Those reflections of paths taken and choices made, big and small, lead to who we are, in ways big and small.

Those decisions can be huge – who we decide to love, to marry, to live with.

Or they can be small – the places we frequent, the habits we hold, the culture we imbibe.

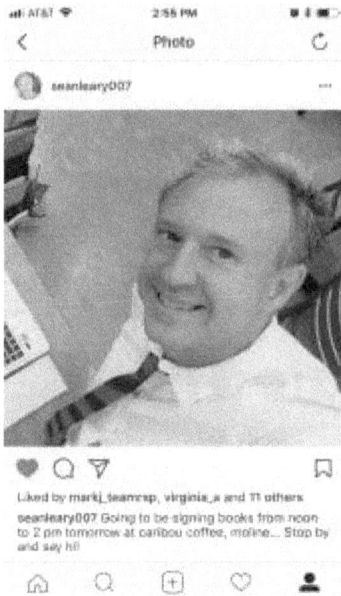

A common sight: Me posting on social media about a book signing at Caribou Coffee.

For more than a decade, Caribou Coffee was a huge part of the mural of my life, and my son's.

And while the closing of a coffee shop may seem small in the larger picture of things, it's still something. Something of resonance. A bit of normalcy that echoes in some subtle nuance of a piece missing from time to time, a routine, a tiny happiness lost.

Not a week went by that Caribou wasn't a part of my life, however small, over the past ten years.

Often, it was selling books, doing book signings and meeting new people. Some people were cool, some were weird. Some bought books. Some told me elaborate stories, just because I was someone to talk to. A few ended up being friends. Some ended up being women I dated. Some were just folks who would smile and wave as they'd walk by from time to time, and for those seconds there was something in that interaction, that compact of normalcy and civility, that brightened our day.

Just as often, and usually at the same time, I was there writing, working on new books and stories for my variety of journalistic enterprises I've been involved in. I'd pick up an iced coffee, or a green tea, my two go-to drinks about 95 percent of the time, and I'd sit there for hours, creating new worlds and alternate realities.

Even more often, I was there in a personal rather than professional capacity, going to BOGO (or as we called it, Laney Boggs – bonus points if you recognize the reference) from 3 to 5 p.m. with my son, Jackson, sitting on the couches, talking, and people-watching as we enjoyed a couple of delicious drinks and some good conversation.

Throughout the past eleven-plus years the coffee shop was open, it was a part of our lives. It was like my "Cheers," a spot where the workers and regulars and I knew each other's names, where we could go to chill out, have some caffeine, and just be comfortable.

It was Jan. 13, 2009, when Caribou opened, and along with it the massive 75,000 square foot HyVee that surrounded it. I was literally one of

My son Jackson and me doing a signing at Caribou Coffee for our children's books we've written together.

the first people to visit both stores, as I was writing for the also now-defunct Rock Island Argus and Moline Dispatch at the time and they sent me to cover the grand opening. I'd never had Caribou before, and quite frankly, had never heard of it. But it was the beginning of a long love affair of coffee-dark exuberance and honey-sweet effervescence.

I introduced myself to the then-manager of Caribou, Tina, to get a quote for my story, and was surprised and delighted to hear that not only did she know who I was from the newspaper, but she was also a fan of my books, particularly my best-seller, the short story collection "Every Number Is Lucky To Someone."

"Would you ever consider doing a book signing here?" she asked.

"Sure!" I replied. "Any time."

And, I certainly lived up to that initial promise.

I did hundreds of signings at Caribou over the years, at pretty much any time, and any day. So much so that it almost became a running leitmotif on my Facebook timeline to see me posting about doing a book signing at Caribou. I once went to a stand-up comedy open mic and one of the comedians made a joke about me being there and not at Caribou. That's how ubiquitous my signings were. Before covid, at least.

Tina would depart as manager, succeeded by Mallory, then Nancy, then Chelsea. But throughout the almost 12 years the store was open, I was there.

My son and I were regulars at Caribou literally since it first opened in January 2009.

And, so was my son, which made the closing even more bittersweet.

My boy, Jackson, wasn't even one-year-old when Caribou opened. I was married at the time to his mother, and our family would go to the HyVee to shop all the time, and every time we would, we would stop at Caribou. So much so that the workers got to know us, our drinks, and our kids. They saw Jackson grow up, and over time, he would develop his favorite drinks and his favorite employees.

When I'd lost my job and was going through my divorce, during the maelstrom of chaos in that year, 2011, Caribou was a small but stable touchstone for my son and me. It was like the spinning top in "Inception" — as long as that little thing kept going, things seemed at least a bit ok. Although many, many things were changing in our lives, and his world was being completely tilted topsy turvy, that was one of the small but significant constants, that acted as a parts of a foundation, cobbled together from disparate parts, to keep the world right side up. The two of us going to get groceries and Caribou drinks were one of those things that remained from the "old life," that no matter what, still had that patina of normalcy to counterbalance anything to the contrary.

His favorite employee during that time was a guy named Erik, who was a gregarious hippie sort, always smiling and happy to chat with my then-three-year-old son, asking him about Thomas the Train or cartoons or whatever was on his mind. Erik and the other folks there would make him little kids-style drinks and it made him feel like a grown up while Dad got his cold-brewed coffee to make it through another day on two or three hours of sleep as a single parent also working and going to grad school.

As my son grew up, and as times changed, and our lives became somewhat less chaotic but busy in different ways, we would spend times there, getting drinks and hanging out. We'd bring a game or soccer cards and play at the tables while we sipped our beverages, or we'd just go

The last signing I did at Caribou Coffee, on March 20 of 2020.

there after school and he would tell me about his day, and we'd talk about soccer, and games, and friends, and life. It was a little home away from home, a cozy nook to just chill out and relax.

There were many other folks who felt the same way, the other regulars I'd see all the time there.

The gent who would show up and draw in his sketch pad; the personal trainer who would have meetings with his clients about diet and exercise programs; the parents whose daughter worked there briefly who would bring their youngest kids around for BOGO on the regular and hang out to let the children draw on the chalkboard table Caribou

233

kept around for kids to exercise their creativity while their parents took a break.

All of those things began to disappear when Caribou announced it was going to be closing.

I first saw the sign, literally, in mid-October.

The store was being shuttered Nov. 15.

We had about a month to say goodbye.

Thankfully, none of the workers would be displaced, they were all either getting other jobs at the HyVee, or, had found other employment.

I hadn't done a signing at Caribou since March 20, the day before Illinois was locked down for covid and everything in our lives changed. I wished I had had the chance to do one more, but it wasn't to be, with all of the safety protocols put in place there. I also wish I had known my last signing was, in fact, the last. I would've cherished it more.

As it was, my son and I continued to frequent Caribou until the day it closed.

A Sunday.

Nov. 15.

As was typical of us on a Sunday, we'd played some soccer, and gone to play some Pokemon Go, and, just before Caribou closed for the last time, we stopped by to get our last drinks.

When I returned from driving across country from California for two weeks, one of the first things I did with my son was go to Caribou, get some drinks, and play our favorite soccer card game. We'll both miss it very much.

We were the last customers there, after I'd been one of the first, almost 12 years before.

And then, even as we were still standing a few feet away from the spot where we'd picked up our last drinks, they closed the register, shut off the machines, and it was gone.

The next day, my son and I stopped by the HyVee, and the Caribou was already literally demolished. Overnight, a crew had come in and leveled it, and in its place, covering the remains, was a massive tarp that would act as camouflage for the workers who would redesign the area, so that eventually there will be no trace of the coffee shop that was once there.

Only memories will remain.

It seems such a small thing, but it's so significant in so many ways.

Not just in it being the end of an era for me personally and professionally. Not just in the fact that an anchor, a small but pleasant constant of my existence, and my son's, and many other people's, is gone.

But in that Caribou is merely one of many businesses like this. One of many, many which have closed this year.

One of the many areas in maps of our experiences, tapestries of time spent, reflections of paths taken in ways big and small, that in total make up who we are, that make up our lives.

The places we frequent, the habits we hold, the culture we imbibe.

Gone.

For more than a decade, Caribou Coffee was a huge part of the mural of my life, and my son's.

And now, no more.

We'll miss it.

next Two Months Crucial

To Recovering Our lives

Nov. 23, 2020

We all want things to get back to normal as quickly as possible. We look at other countries like Australia and New Zealand and they're already having big sporting events and concerts and leading normal lives again.

I want the same. I want to have my jobs and income fully back, I want to be able to go out and see friends, I want my son and his friends to be able to play soccer games again, I want my friends who own businesses to be able to open them up and keep them open.

And that can happen here, but it's going to take some sacrifice and some work.

And now's the time to do it.

3. Where There May Be Bad News Ahead

Here, the metro areas where new cases are rising the fastest, on a population-adjusted basis:

Where new cases are increasing fastest

The Quad-Cities has moved up to number 6 nationwide on the worst covid hot spots in the entire United States.

We're on a precipice here with the one-two-three punch of Thanksgiving, Christmas/other winter solstice holidays, and New Year's Eve coming up.

Now, this can go a couple of ways.

Worst case scenario, millions of people continue to not care, don't wear masks, don't act responsibly, and generally go nuts the same way the folks did when thousands of them went to the Sturgis Motorcycle Rally.

And, what happens then is what happened in the aftermath of the Sturgis Motorcycle Rally, which led to North and South Dakota leading the entire world in covid cases and deaths per capita right now.

That's what could happen over the next two months, and if that happens, that'll spill over into the beginning of 2021, and we'll be in a horrible spot early next year going into the spring, making things even worse than they were last spring.

Which likely means no school, businesses closed, no spring sports, and no concerts or anything likewise until late summer at the earliest.

Or, we could go another way.

People can chill out on the next two months and be smart, safe, and responsible. Don't go out and get nuts on Blackout Wednesday and Black Friday. Be responsible getting together with families for Thanksgiving and holiday celebrations. Don't go out and get hammered and turn New Year's Eve into a super-spreader event.

Yeah, yeah, I know it sucks. I'm not a big fan of it either. But I'm a bigger fan of that than I am of being in lockdown through early 2021 and into the spring and still dealing with this mess into summer of next year.

The choice is ours.

We'll see what the future holds.

Even This Year, There Are Things To Be Thankful For

Nov. 27, 2020

It was a surreal Thanksgiving.

My ex-wife and I alternate years on holidays, and it's always strange and depressing for me when I don't get to see my son on those days, especially when I'm reminded of the fun times we had the year before in the memories section of social media.

This year was even more downcast, given the dark cloud of covid. Whereas in previous years when I was without my son, I would go to visit family or friends, or have people over to my house, this year there was none of that. I wasn't going to be visiting my family, nor would there be my usual open door to people to stop by and hang, partaking in the way-too-much food I would typically make for the event, chill out in the living room and have a beverage or two while watching sports on the TV all day.

Instead, the day before Thanksgiving, I started to come down sick with something, which this year is always accompanied by a sense of foreboding.

Symptoms? Little bit of a sore throat. Terrible headache. Aches and pains and tired.

Could it be covid? Not sure. Could it be nothing more than a sinus infection or just being worn down from working too hard and burning the candle at both ends? Not sure.

At any rate, after dropping my son off at his mom's Wednesday evening, I basically went home and crashed. Slept through most of the night, other than an hour or two past midnight when I woke up and drank some water and watched a couple episodes of "Better Call Saul" in bed. Then crashed again, hoping that I would feel better in the morning and wouldn't have to consider the possibility of this being the beginning of something worse.

And as I fell asleep, I remember distinctly having a negative attitude, in general, about my situation, about the country, about the world. This year has been terrible in so many ways, that regardless of any holiday designation, it made it difficult for me to feel thankful about much of anything, even though there was a part of me, a much more optimistic side, that realized that I did have much for which to be appreciative.

And, thankfully (pun intended), when I woke up, finally, at around 1:45 in the afternoon the next day after about 14 hours of sleep, I felt fine, and it was obvious that it was just my body finally telling me to chill the hell out after too many nights of staying up working until 4 a.m. and then waking up early the next day to drive my machine into the red once more. This has been typical of me since I was a teenager, and I'll usually hit that wall, take a day or two to sleep a ton and recoup, and then get back at my typical frenetic lifestyle. At any rate, I was happy that when I woke, I felt far better than I had the night before.

I texted out Happy Thanksgiving to various friends, answered texts, and had some breakfast before going out into the world to experience the day.

I've been determined for the last few years to never go to a store or any business on Thanksgiving. I've long felt that by churning money towards businesses on holidays, it just encourages the corporations that own them to see that there's profitability in forcing their workers to show up on days when they should be respected and considered and given a day off. So, after taking a walk and doing some work around the house, I headed out for a drive, to play Pokemon Go and head to a couple of parks just to get out of the house for some fresh air.

Out of curiosity I drove by a few businesses that are typically open on the holiday, and was pleasantly surprised to see Starbucks, Target, and Kohls, were closed, along with various other locally-owned places along John Deere Road in Rock Island. I was happy to see that, knowing it meant that people who work there were able to stay home and enjoy a day off with their families.

Around 7 p.m. I found myself driving up into the parking lot of a local church, which also happens to be a Pokestop where a raid was taking place (if you play Pokemon Go, you'll know what I'm talking about; if you don't, essentially Pokemon Go makes the entire world a virtual gamescape with various locations acting as spots to play the games. I got into it because my son was playing it and it's something we continue to share; it's a fun video game and it encourages me to get my butt out of the house and take walks and drives in the winter, which is a good thing given that I work from home and during covid, that means my usual coffee shops and other remote office spots are closed, leaving me more of a hermit than usual).

There was another car there already, a beat-up pickup truck.

Now, a lot of times, there are multiple players who show up for raids, and I assumed this to be the case with the truck, although when I went into the arena to do the raid, nobody was there. So, I thought, despite the church being closed, maybe these people are somehow affiliated with the church. I didn't give it much thought. It's a church on a main thoroughfare; I hardly thought anything nefarious was taking place under the spotlights next to a busy street.

As the raid was getting over with, and I was getting ready to leave, they drove by me, and stopped by my car. I saw that the two people in the car were an older man, who looked to be around his fifties, and a young girl, probably no older than 10.

They rolled down the window, and called out to me, still in my car. I rolled down my window a bit to hear them, figuring a guy in his fifties with a 10-year-old wasn't about to attempt to carjack me, not that my decade-old Nissan Versa was all that tempting of a target.

"Are you with the church?" the guy asked.

I figured he was. I figured he was going to ask what I was doing there. It's happened before. So I held up my phone and showed him the screen, on which were an array of colorful creatures amidst a bright background.

"No," I said, "I'm just here playing Pokemon Go."

"Oh, ok," he said, sounding downtrodden. "So there's nobody from the church here?"

"No, not that I'm aware of, they look closed," I said.

"Ok," he said, putting the truck into reverse and getting ready to go. "Sorry to bother you. We're homeless and were hoping someone was here."

Then he rolled up his window, and took off, before I could even reply.

And as he left, I could see in the bed of his truck, a small refrigerator, and various boxes, strapped in to the back of the truck bed, so as to not fall off.

Now, 2020 has certainly not been a great year for me. Nor has it been for a great number of people whom I consider friends, and others who I don't even know personally. I've lost a number of jobs this year and had my income cut by more than 60 percent due to covid and its negative impact on the arts world and the various other job fields (teaching, public relations, etc.) I occupy. Our website here has lost its advertising revenue, due to the various shutdowns, although we continue to shoulder on. Dozens of folks I know who also own local businesses have had to shut them down. Dozens of folks I know are unemployed. All of this is through no fault of our own.

But at least we're not homeless.

At least we're not driving around in a beat-up truck with our kids on Thanksgiving night, looking for churches or anywhere that might be open to lend a hand.

And I'm certain that's what this guy was really doing. I'm a cynical sort, and I tend to be very dubious in regard to motives and the gaps between what people say and what they do. I've been hit up by various scam artists and con-men, panhandlers and swindlers over the years.

This guy didn't ask me for anything. He just wanted to know if I was possibly affiliated with the church where he had gone with what I would assume was his daughter, to find shelter for the night.

Then they drove off.

I didn't see them again after that.

I drove around to a few other places, a few other stops, called my son during that time, because I missed him. I called just to talk to him, and he joined in on the game remotely, so that even though we weren't together in person, we were still able to share that time together.

Then I went home.

And as I walked in, I realized that, regardless of any misfortunes or difficulties I had, there were ways in which I was blessed, in which I had reasons to be thankful.

And maybe, in that way, this was probably the most appropriate thanksgiving I could've had this year after all.

Elliot Page Has A Right To Be Whoever They Want To

Dec. 11, 2020

This week, the "Juno" and "Umbrella Academy" star formerly known as Ellen Page made an announcement that they are transgender, want to heretofore be known as Elliot Page, and that their pronouns now are he/they.

I remember exactly where I was when I first read this.

Because it was only a couple days ago.

Upon reading this, I took a deep breath, had a drink of my iced coffee, flipped back over to my other window on my computer, and went back to work because I had things to do.

It never really struck me beyond that.

246

Sure, I really liked "Juno," and I really like "Umbrella Academy." The enjoyment of both had an impact on my life, however small and transient.

On the other hand, I had heard that Elliot had been gay, and that didn't really have any impact on me either. The same way this doesn't. It's not like I've ever met Elliot Page, nor was I planning on hitting on them with any romantic intent. I'm not transgender. I'm not gay. So, really, this literally had pretty much zero impact on my life.

All I thought was, "Good for him/them. I hope they're happy."

Of course, that's not the attitude of some people.

On the far right, predictably, we saw a trio of reactions – one was ridicule (paging Steven Crowder), the other was outrage about the politics of the left in regard to it, and the third was religious indignation because the biblical translation was mistakenly changed from pedophile to homosexual in 1946, and so some people think this is a sin, I guess? (Although this reaction of a conversion therapy victim was also trending, and sad.)

On the far left, which likewise excels at creating tempests in even the smallest teapots, Elliot was being attacked by lesbians and lesbian supporters because, I guess, by him transitioning into a him it somehow diminished his, formerly her, lesbianism? Is that right? I don't know. I'm confused, and quite frankly, my dears, I don't give a damn enough to figure it out.

Hi friends, I want to share with you that I am trans, my pronouns are he/they and my name is Elliot. I feel lucky to be writing this. To be here. To have arrived at this place in my life.

I feel overwhelming gratitude for the incredible people who have supported me along this journey. I can't begin to express how remarkable it feels to finally love who I am enough to pursue my authentic self. I've been endlessly inspired by so many in the trans community. Thank you for your courage, your generosity and ceaselessly working to make this world a more inclusive and compassionate place. I will offer whatever support I can and continue to strive for a more loving and equal society.

I also ask for patience. My joy is real, but it is also fragile. The truth is, despite feeling profoundly happy right now and knowing how much privilege I carry, I am also scared. I'm scared of the invasiveness, the hate, the "jokes" and of violence. To be clear, I am not trying to dampen a moment that is joyous and one that I celebrate, but I want to address the full picture. The statistics are staggering. The discrimination towards trans people is vile, insidious and cruel, resulting in horrific consequences. In 2020 alone it has been reported that at least 40 transgender people have been murdered, the majority of which were Black and Latinx trans women. To the political leaders who work to criminalize trans health care and deny our right to exist and to all of those with a massive platform who continue to spew hostility towards the trans community: you have blood on your hands. You unleash a fury of vile and demeaning rage that lands on the shoulders of the trans community, a community in which 40% of trans adults report attempting suicide. Enough is enough. You aren't being "canceled," you are hurting people. I am one of these people and we won't be silent in the face of your attacks.

I love that I am trans. And I love that I am queer. And the more I hold myself close and fully embrace who I am, the more I dream, the more my heart grows and the more I thrive. To all trans people who deal with harassment, self-loathing, abuse and the threat of violence every day: I see you, I love you and I will do everything I can to change this world for the better.

Thank you for reading this.

All my love,

Elliot

Elliot Page's statement on social media.

Ya know, I'm trying to recall when this intense concern about everyone else's life and business began. Certainly, gossip and celebrity fluff magazines have existed since there have been celebrities, but it's really flared in the last decade or two as the internet has prospered.

And I really don't like it.

Because quite frankly, I don't think it should be anyone else's business what someone does in their private life as long as it doesn't impact anyone else.

If the former Ellen Page wants to be known as Elliot Page and be called by a different pronoun or seen as whatever sexuality they want, then why do you care?

Seriously.

I'll bet probably 99 percent of the people writing about this, pro and con, myself included, HAVE NEVER MET ELLIOT PAGE AND THEY HAVE ABSOLUTELY NO DIRECT IMPACT UPON OUR LIVES WHATSOEVER.

For people to be getting so bent out of shape about this is FREAKING MORONIC.

Listen, I could give a flying f if someone wants to be called freakin' F You Yankee Bluejeans and identify as a Berzerker if it has no bearing on my life or my son's life, and no bearing on my business, health or financial situation.

My position in regard to Elliot Page, as my position is in regard to pretty much anything is this:

Do what YOU want to do, and be who YOU want to be in order to pursue your own happiness. And I wish you well. Period. Do whatever you want as long as it doesn't negatively impact on other people, especially me. Once it negatively impacts upon me, THEN it's my business, and I'll certainly have a response to it.

But until then, I don't give a damn. You do you. Be happy. Live your life.

Pursue your own path, your own love, your own bliss. Because damn it, we're only inhabiting this matrix for a short time, so let's enjoy the ride.

And I think more people should follow that credo, and take that advice to heart in their own lives.

Because honestly, the more people that do THAT, that pursue happiness, that concentrate on their own lives and their own bliss, the better off this world IS going to be, and THAT is actually going to end up having a measurable ripple effect upon the rest of us.

So, good on ya, Elliot Page. I wish you happiness and love in your life, and I hope it translates into you continuing to make good work on the big and small screens.

But regardless of whether it does or not, I hope you personally have happiness in your life. And if anyone out there is inspired by you, or is made to feel less alone by you and your announcement, that's fantastic. I wish the same for them as well. And, for that matter, I wish the same for all of you out there.

Except for Tom Brady.

To hell with that guy.

●●●●●●●●●●●●●●●●●slghvl0

Now Is The Time To Take

Action For Covid Recovery

Dec. 16, 2020

Some call me a pessimist.

Some call me a cynic.

Some call me the space cowboy, some call me the gangster of love.

I prefer to think of myself as, no, not Maurice, but, rather, a pragmatist.

A realist.

And realistically, I don't see the next few months going well in terms of covid-19.

Today, Kim Reynolds is going to talk about potentially pulling back restrictions she put in place a month ago in regard to the pandemic ripping its way through the Midwest, and especially Iowa.

Many think she's going to pull back the restrictions.

I don't think she should.

I know everyone wants to get back to normal and wants everything to be fantastic again, as if nothing ever happened, and believe me, so do I, but I don't see it happening for a while.

That's not based on wanton negativity, it's based on data, facts and extrapolation of both.

Covid numbers throughout the United States are insane and we as a country have just become numb and dumb to them to dull the impact. Among the top 10 days marking the one-day greatest losses of life in the history of this country, the majority of them are deaths due to covid.

Since Iowa and Illinois went to mitigation measures, Iowa on Nov. 17, and Illinois on Nov. 20, the numbers in both states have slowly sloped downwards.

In Illinois, Governor JB Pritzker is seeing that as a positive sign that the mitigations he put into place are working, and in response to the fact that numbers everywhere are still substantial, he's keeping them in place. People may not like it, but from a logical perspective, it's the right thing to do. He's found something that's working at keeping them at bay and actually reducing cases during a time of soaring infections, and so he's continuing on the path to keep those numbers hopefully at bay and continuing to go down.

Iowa's Kim Reynolds is another story. Iowa's mitigations as they stand aren't as restrictive as Illinois, and the number of infections and deaths in Iowa reflects the fact that Iowa has long been slow to come up with mitigations. Like Illinois, since their mitigations have been put into place, the number has been sloping downwards, but that doesn't change the fact that Iowa's number of infections has been consistently three times or more larger than Illinois' number, despite Illinois having roughly four times the population of Iowa. The death tolls are usually roughly the same in terms of daily numbers, which, again, does not look well for Iowa given that their population number is far lower than Illinois and their population density is nowhere near as high.

JB Pritzker at his press conference yesterday.

Reynolds announced last week that she's slowly easing up on mitigations and looking at scaling them back as soon as today. If she does, expect it to be a disaster, because without mitigations put forth in some form, regardless of state, the upcoming months are going to be a mess.

Right now we're starting to see increasing numbers due to the huge number of people who didn't pay attention to mitigations and the common sense requests in place – masks, social distancing, stay at home if you can, etc. – during the Thanksgiving holiday.

If you think that's bad, just wait.

In less than ten days, we see Christmas, and within this time are a number of other religious and secular holidays as well, offering people the opportunity to get together.

Then there's New Year's Eve, which is going to invite a number of parties and huge gatherings into the mix.

It usually takes 2-3 weeks for infection numbers to spike after these types of gatherings. Well, 2-3 weeks after Thanksgiving takes us to mid-December. Then 2-3 weeks after the Christmas and New Year's Week takes us into mid-January.

Then there's a brief respite and Valentine's Day pops up, which again invites people to disregard any protocols.

Take that out 2-3 weeks and we're into March.

Then mid-March is another big drinking and social gathering holiday, St. Patrick's Day. Not to mention spring break for various colleges going on throughout March.

Take that out two weeks, and there's April.

And right there on April 4 is Easter.

So throw another couple of weeks on there after people disregard protocols for Easter, and we're in mid-late April.

Almost May.

Four months from now.

All the sudden, we're here in mid-December, looking at another four-five months of dealing with this.

We're looking at four-five months of people getting sick, people who had previously blown it off realizing it's not a whole lot of fun to get it, people filling up hospitals, people dying.

And people dying because of all the covid patients in the hospitals.

That's one of the things that gets consistently overlooked in this.

Sure, the mortality rate is relatively low. Sure, the majority of the people dying are older. But those folks deserve medical care too. Those folks don't deserve to be left to die. And when they come to a hospital, they're going to get that care, and need to take up a hospital bed to get it.

Now, when they take up that hospital bed, that's one less hospital bed open for other treatable health matters that are in urgent need of medical care. Heart attacks. Strokes. Car accidents. Various other maladies that need ICU and ER care. What happens if covid patients are taking up all the beds and there's a flurry of people coming in from an accident? What if there are beds being taken up by people with other injuries or maladies and suddenly there's a covid surge, where do those covid patients go, especially if they are older?

Those are the things that <u>doctors and nurses keep telling me when I interview them about this</u>. It's not just covid, it's the domino effect of covid that's causing a crisis within the hospitals, and the fact that people are disregarding that factor.

And that's not even taking into account the other factors of covid: People being out of work, businesses shuttering their doors temporarily, businesses shutting their doors permanently, kids being out of school and experiencing another epidemic of academic failures which is being documented across the country. How many kids who are already academically or socially challenged are being pushed even further behind by this? How many people in poverty are being shoved down deeper into a hole by it?

It's tough to say this could've all been prevented, because it's impossible to predict a virus. We live in a vast country and odds are there was always going to be a virulent spread.

However, it could've, and should've, been better. It could've, and should've, been handled better. By those in authority, and the general population. It wasn't. It hasn't been.

But it still could be.

People have had the time to see what's going on. People have had the opportunity to get the facts. People have had the opportunity to experience the impact themselves. And hopefully, people have changed their opinions and become more careful and smart about this.

It's really not that big of a sacrifice to wear a mask. It's really not that big of a deal to socially distance. To cut down on your social exposure. To be smart about your interactions. And, here's something that rarely gets mentioned but should more often: To take proven measures to strengthen your immune system to make it more difficult for you to get and spread the virus.

We've got an opportunity here to turn things around. Yes, the first round of the vaccine is here, being given first to health care providers, as it should be. But it's going to take a while for it to get out into the general public. And even when it does, only half of the people in the U.S. are saying they'll definitely take it, and a full quarter of the population is saying that they definitely won't.

We're still in for a bumpy ride for a while here. But it can be better if we can all learn from the mistakes of the past year and build upon the successes.

I hope that the numbers get better. I hope that the mitigations work. I hope that people follow the mitigations and do the right things, and they're as sick of all this crap as I am, and decide to hell with it, let's buckle down and make the sacrifices and mask up, social distance, chill on the big gatherings, and get this done, and get beyond this so that we can get our normal lives back.

But will that happen?

Or will the next four to five months play out like a roller coaster, with a series of dips rolling up fast into spikes following all the holidays coming up, and people continuing to disregard mitigation measures?

What do you think?

●●●●●●●●●●●●●●●●●slghvl0

This Year Has Sucked, Let

People Have Their McRibs

Dec. 18, 2020

I was scrolling through my news feed on Facebook today, as I am wont to do when I want to incrementally lose faith in humanity, and I stopped briefly on a posting by someone trying to make themselves look far more hip and cool than they actually are.

I know, I know, hard to pin that one down when it comes to social media! You'll never guess who I'm talking about when you've got 80 million people to choose from there…

Anyway, the person was making a comment about a certain fast food item that some people (not myself, but some people), profoundly enjoy. They post about it. They revel in its return. They write with glee about its magnificence to them.

This person was scalding the fans of said item, which is within their right to express their opinion, but they ended it by saying "You're all wrong for thinking this is any good. It's nowhere as good as you think it is."

Now, of course, upon reading this, my inclination was to instantly message this person.

Because, well, if they can read minds with that much accuracy and are that certain about the vagaries of chance and choice, well, I want next week's lottery numbers from them.

They didn't message back.

And so, a little tear trickled down my cheek, like that Native American guy in that old commercial.

Then, I turned and walked away, with my backpack slung over my shoulder, as the Incredible Hulk Lonely Man Theme played in the background, and I strode into the distance, to my destiny…

A destiny that, for the moment, involved me writing this column.

And one of the reasons I wanted to write this column is that, for one thing, NOBODY can ever say someone is wrong for thinking a food item is good. It's an opinion. It's a matter of preference.

You can jokingly say that pineapple on pizza is an abomination against God and man, but you'd be wrong, because it's a delicacy of the Gods and a gift to man. However, in that case, both of us are right — for ourselves.

I love pineapple on pizza. You may hate it. But I can't say you're wrong, and you can't say I'm wrong. It's completely subjective and a matter of opinion.

The same way this person can't say with such venom that people are wrong for liking this certain foodstuff that rhymes with McHibb, and they can't say that it's not as good as they think it is, because for one, how can you read their minds to find out exactly how good they think it is, and for another, that's just like, their opinion, man.

And when it comes down to it, it's really kind of a superficial thing.

And it's also something that, especially in a time like this, and a year like this, we should just back off and let people have their small moments of joy regardless of how we feel about them personally.

Because not only do those little things sometimes mean a lot during times that are difficult, but in the big picture, those superficialities often don't mean a whole hell of a lot in accurately judging someone's character.

For example, as you all know, I make fun of Nickelback as much as the next guy. Especially if the next guy isn't Chad Kroeger.

But the fact is, one of the best relationships I had was with a woman who was one of the kindest people I've met, and she loved Nickelback.

I've also known really cool people and had relationships with really cool women who have LOVED Michael Bolton, Mariah Carey, Matchbox 20, Garth Brooks, and various other musicians who make me cringe.

Conversely, I've had horrible relationships and encountered really shitty people who had the exact same musical and entertainment tastes as me.

When it comes down to it, people have a right to enjoy what makes them happy, and it's not up to me or anyone else to condemn them or judge them for that. I might vehemently disagree with their choices, I might consider it a form of torture to join them in engaging in them, but what's REALLY important is if someone is a good person, has good character, and is nice and respectful to you as a human being. THAT is worth a hell of a lot more than being able to agree on music and TV choices.

Trust me on this one.

Also, it's really not up to you, or your right, to tell someone what they can and can't like, or to make statements like "that's not as good as you think it is." Everyone is entitled to their own opinions, their own preferences, and their own things that bring them joy. And in this world, which can be pretty damn shitty, we need to embrace those things that bring us joy.

So if you really love someone, you really want to see them happy, let them have their Nickelback. Let them have their Olive Garden. Let them have their "Friends."

And yes, Goddamn it, let them have their McRibs.

Because if there's one thing I've learned through all the relationships I've had, it's that I'd much rather be with someone who's kind, and nice, and cool, and upbeat, with good character, who has completely different entertainment tastes than me, than the opposite.

A Christmas Classic Takes

On Greater Significance

Dec. 25, 2020

It was late 1984, and Boomtown Rats front man Bob Geldof was sitting down to watch a bit of telly as the calendar began to turn towards the holidays.

However, what he saw that evening was anything but festive.

Geldof watched as a documentary news program detailed the horrible starving and suffering going on in Africa due to incredible droughts and oppression. And as he watched, he was moved to tears, sorrow, and finally, action.

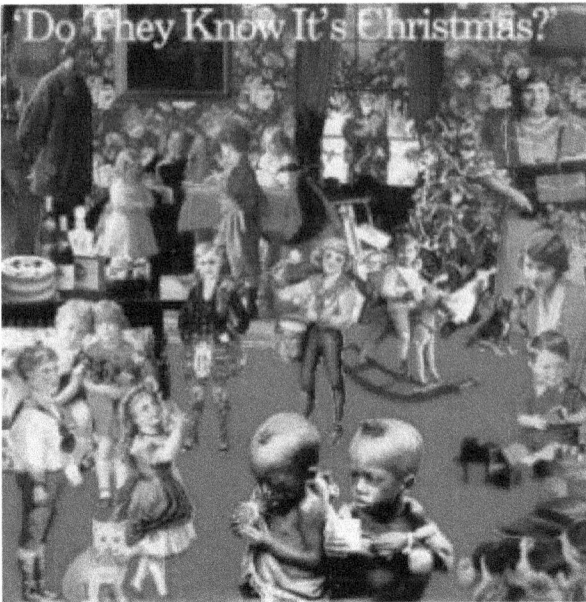

'Do They Know It's Christmas?'

He knew he had to do something to help, but just donating money himself seemed so small, so insignificant. How could he do something larger? Finally, he had the idea, and the structure for a song, and a movement, that would literally change the world.

Geldof called up his friend Midge Ure of Ultravox and the two set about to quickly penning one of the most stirring and beautiful Christmas songs of all time, "Do They Know It's Christmas?"

For the recording of the song, the duo hit the phones to call up every pop star they knew, and to tell those pop stars to call their friends, to hastily put together a massive group — Band Aid — to record the track and get it in stores before Christmas to raise as much money as possible for the starving people of Africa.

Remarkably, they got an incredible all-star lineup of talent, and the biggest rock and pop stars in Britain and worldwide at the time — members of the bands Duran Duran, U2, Wham!, Culture Club, The Police, Kool and the Gang, Spandau Ballet, and dozens of others, joined together to record a song and video which would go on to become the biggest-selling single of all time in Britain and several other countries around the world. It would go on to spark a massive movement to help the people of Africa that would lead to the unforgettable Live Aid concert the next year, and would directly lead to various other movements, from USA For Africa to Farm Aid.

As Geldof put it at the time, "We made compassion fashionable."

His co-songwriter and partner in the project, Midge Ure, echoed those sentiments, saying, "It made caring cool again."

And as we live through our own difficult year, our own difficult time in this world, perhaps nothing could be more important this holiday season than to once more, make compassion fashionable.

This year has been unbelievably difficult in so many ways. We've seen thousands of people killed by a pandemic, and our societies and lives disrupted in profound and meaningful ways by the pandemic and its symptoms in shutting down businesses and wide swaths of our lives. We've seen social upheaval, protests and riots and massive demonstrations, both peaceful and violent.

There's been a horrible schism that's widened between people along various political, religious and social lines, grown larger and deeper by those who profit and prosper in fomenting divisions among us.

And it's become fashionable to be a jerk, to not care, to be rude and unsympathetic, to be an asshole.

It's time for that to change.

To be certain, that plague of disdain and cold uncaring hasn't been all-encompassing.

There are plenty of people who have been a light in the darkness, who have steadfastly been a source of positivity and compassion during this time.

Healthcare workers and providers have been especially crucial.

Teachers have been essential.

And really, anyone who has recognized that almost all of us are in the same boat and shown some compassion and understanding to others has helped in some way, however small, to make things a little better during this time.

There have also been people who have stood up for, and fought for, the downtrodden, and those suffering. There are those who have stood on the side of truth, of positive evolution, of logic and common sense, and an escape from the cages of tribalism that only end up dividing, that only end up making it worse for the people who are suffering.

That courage, that caring, should be recognized.

That should be praised.

That should be highlighted.

That should be made fashionable, made cool.

It's time to make compassion fashionable again.

It's time to make caring cool.

Not just today, not just during the holiday season, but in all the days moving forward.

Merry Christmas, and happy holidays…

facebook Is Dying. And

Good Riddance

Dec. 26, 2020

There was a time, around 2006, when EVERYONE was on MySpace.

The social media platform was ubiquitous, especially if you were under 30. Everyone you knew was on it, everyone was having fun on it. And to be honest, it was a really fun time in society and online life and MySpace was the pinnacle of that.

MySpace wasn't political, it wasn't full of conspiracy theories and hate speech and ridiculous falsehoods, and vicious arguments and people being blocked. It was largely about people posting fun pictures of themselves and sharing music that they enjoyed, and then people generally commenting in a friendly and civil fashion.

You could rank your top friends, and it was fun to see who would be up there on a frequent basis.

It just seemed like a much more fun and lighthearted time.

And then along came Facebook.

Like so many others, I started up a Facebook profile in 2007 just for the heck of it. After all, at that point, every time a new social media platform popped up, I would start up a profile on it, because social media wasn't big business, it was something fun and escapist. Nobody really took it seriously. (And yes, somewhere out there I have a xanga.)

Tom would never have done this. He only wanted us to have fun.

Flash forward more than a decade.

MySpace is long gone. The shell of it is still there, but it hasn't been relevant in more than a decade.

And as for Facebook?

It's feeling an awful lot like MySpace was in 2009 — not in terms of content, because MySpace then was still 1,000 times better than Facebook is now in regard to that — but in terms of it being a dead man walking. The only difference being, Facebook's zombie is still waiting for its social media Negan to completely annihilate it.

That Negan has yet to emerge, but it's out there. It's just a matter of time, and that time is probably down to about a year or two at most.

Facebook is dying.

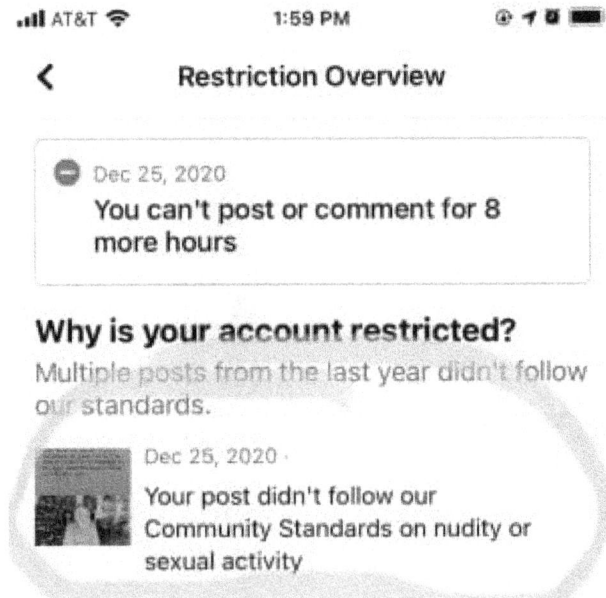

.ıll AT&T 🛜   1:59 PM   @ ⤴ 🔋 ▬

‹   **Restriction Overview**

⊖ Dec 25, 2020
  You can't post or comment for 8 more hours

Why is your account restricted?

Multiple posts from the last year didn't follow our standards.

Dec 25, 2020 ·

Your post didn't follow our Community Standards on nudity or sexual activity

Yup.

And, good riddance.

For the most part, it's grown incredibly tedious. I used to love Facebook when it first emerged. Because it still had some of the fun of MySpace attached. You could share pictures and stories, and posts, and although it was missing the really fun musical elements and the "top five" of MySpace, it was more expansive and interesting.

But especially in the last four years, it's become a dumpster fire, and as the company has become more greedy and allocated more of its editorial decisions to robots instead of people, the choices to "ban" people have become increasingly ludicrous.

Just this weekend I was notified I was banned from posting on Facebook for 24 hours.

Why?

Due to a post not following their "community standards on nudity or sexual activity."

That content?

I shared a story from QuadCities.com about a local couple who received a surprise holiday phone call from Dick Van Dyke.

DICK Van Dyke.

Yes.

THAT'S why Facebook banned me for 24 hours.

Apparently because of the name "DICK VAN DYKE."

271

Even Dick Van Dyke can't believe this bullshit.

In the meantime, Facebook has become a cesspool of disinformation and asinine conspiracy theories. If you can think of a ridiculous chunk of conspiratorial crap that's emerged in the past few years — everything from pizzagate to QAnon — it's been spread to the masses on Facebook. The platform has become an intellectual disease hotbed of stupidity and ignorance.

And people are quickly recognizing that.

Sure, we still acknowledge that there are a lot of people on Facebook, and so we use it to promote our events and business interests.

But more and more, very few people I know are spending significant time on there.

Most people, myself included, go on there to promote their things — maybe they throw in a few posts beforehand to boost up the algorithm and get into people's news feeds, and THEN we promote our things — and then they leave it alone.

Another incredibly offensive Dick pic.

Most people I know — and I know a lot of folks who tend to be on the cutting edge of new trends and ahead of the curve on social waves — have pretty much abandoned it other than to use it for utilitarian purposes. And those utilitarian purposes are only going to be relevant as long as Facebook holds on to its status as the only major game in town in regard to social media audience. Once the tipping point hits — and it will, soon — in which Facebook begins to fade in terms of audience, people are going to start abandoning it in droves, and it's going to end up becoming basically what MySpace is now. It'll still be there, but nobody will really be on it in an active way.

Facebook is only relevant because nothing has emerged to challenge it on a macroeconomic or macro-social scale. But give it time, because we're already seeing large groups of people leave and avoid it in droves.

Parler, the new social media site geared towards conservatives, has drawn a big crowd of those politically leaning folks away from Facebook; TikTok and Snapchat have pulled everyone Gen Z; Instagram and Snapchat are pulling more millenials; so the signs are there that people are looking for other avenues and they're sick of Facebook and its crap.

If something comes along to pull Gen X, it's all over. Because most boomers could take or leave it, and many are only on there to keep in touch with their younger family members and friends.

Mary Poppins would be very disappointed in you, Mark Zuckerberg.

And honestly, I look forward to that day, which will be coming soon.

Unlike MySpace, which I still miss to this day, I don't foresee me having wistful memories for the halcyon days of Facebook. It's always seemed like little more than a corporate entity which was forced upon us because we had little choice in the matter. It's like the only dive bar in a small town. It's a hellhole, but, hey, where else are you gonna go to see your friends?

Personally, I enjoy Instagram, with its panoramas of beautiful and interesting photos and stories, and TikTok, with its goofy videos, a whole lot more.

None of them are MySpace though.

And wouldn't it be ironic, then, if it was a return of MySpace that killed off Facebook?

Doubtful. As much as I, and many other Gen Xers would love to see it.

But something will. And soon. The writing is on the wall, in big block letters, for anyone to see it.

Except for maybe Dick Van Dyke. I hear he's been banned.

Other Books By Sean Leary

The Arimathean (novel)

The Blood of Destiny (novel)

Black Knight Apocalypse (novel)

Luna Death Trigger (novel)

DisIntegration (novel)

Does The Shed Skin Know It Was Once A Snake? (short stories)

Every Number Is Lucky To Someone

(short stories)

My Life As A Freak Magnet

(short stories)

Exorcising Ghosts

(graphic novel)

Here Comes The Goot!

(children's/beginning readers)

Go, Racecars, Go!

(children's/beginning readers)

Nine Little Penguin Ninjas

(children's/beginning readers)

Baby Bird

(children's/beginning readers)

We Are All Characters

(children's/beginning readers)

All My Best Adventures Are With You

(children's/beginning readers)

Beautiful Remnants of Chaotic Failures

(poetry)

Danger Maps

(poetry)

Every Broken Heart Creates The Pieces That Will Pave The Way To The Place Your Heart Will Call Home

(poetry)

Tricks of the Light

(poetry)

The Soft Venom of Promise

(poetry)

The Night Universal

(poetry)

There Is Truth In The Untamed Beat of a Heart

(poetry)

We Are Shadows In The Absence of Light

(poetry)

Magnets & Mysteries, Soft Curves & Comets

(poetry)

Infinite Sky

(poetry)

Physics & Beauty

(poetry)

Dark Equinox

(graphic novel)

The Ink In The Well

(graphic novel)

Dream States

(graphic novel)

Valentine Cords

(graphic novel)

Spyder

(graphic novel)

Sean Leary's Greatest Hits, volume one

(humor)

Sean Leary's Greatest Hits, volume two

(humor)

Sean Leary's Greatest Hits, volume three

(humor)

Sean Leary's Greatest Hits, volume four

(humor)

Sean Leary's Greatest Hits, volume five

(humor)

Sean Leary's Greatest Hits, volume six

(humor)

Sean Leary's Greatest Hits, volume seven

(humor)

Sean Leary's Greatest Hits, volume eight

(humor)

Sean Leary's Greatest Hits, volume nine

(humor)

Sean Leary's Greatest Hits, volume ten

(humor)

Your Favorite Band

(stageplay / screenplay)

Dingo Boogaloo

(stageplay / screenplay)

Rock City Live!

(stageplay / screenplay)

My Life As A Freak Magnet: The Scripts

(stageplay / screenplay)

Shots To The Heart

(stageplay)

Advice to My Son

(life stories and positive parenting)

Subliminal Cartography

(novel)

I Don't Have The Map

(poetry)

For more writing and more information, see
www.seanleary.com.

Hey, stop reading.

Go find another book, like one of those many fine Sean Leary books listed on those pages just before this one...

Enjoy the trip...

www.ingramcontent.com/pod-product-compliance
Lightning Source LLC
Chambersburg PA
CBHW020847090426
42736CB00008B/273